CHOICE PUBLISHING INC.

PRESENTS

The

Providential

Doberman

1

Lessons Learned from a

Rescued Dog

And Other Great Animals'

Jeanie E. A. Notti-Fullerton

As inspired by

Miley Anne Fullerton, PhD

Dedication

This book is dedicated to all my beloved pets, past, present, and future. I am the tender-heart I am because of the lessons I was taught early on by animals of all sorts. And to my patient husband, Marty, who has been put to the test repeatedly and who loves animals more now and is a better person for the animals we've had in our lives. And most importantly I dedicate this writing to my God, Jehovah, for providentially granting me the blessing of Miley, a wounded waif, who came to heal my heart, my body, and my spirit.

Prologue

On October 11th, 2008 I lost one of the dearest, most loyal and most appreciative friends I've ever had. The intensity of the pain with this loss is beyond description, but when I gave Miley "permission" to let go of her tired and dis-eased body, "permission" to leave me, I told her I had to stay for awhile longer because I needed to tell her story. This book is Miley's legacy, in the tradition of the 19th century American classic *Beautiful Joe*, a book written through the eyes of an abused dog that was rescued. Miley's book is written through the eyes of the people who rescued her, whose lives she forever changed for the better because of the joy she brought us.

"However, ask, please, the domestic animals
and they will instruct you."

Job 12:7

Table of Contents

Providence (prov'i dens), n. 1. the foreseeing care and guardianship of God over His creatures. 2. (cap) God, esp. when conceived as omnisciently directing the universe and the affairs of man with wise benevolence. 3. a manifestation of divine care or direction. --Webster's Encyclopedic Unabridged Dictionary of the English Language

Chapter 1

Lucky

"Lucky" -- it would be so interesting to know how she got that name. By all appearances she had been anything but lucky to this point.

December 27th, 2002. Winters in Montana are a mixed bag of weather, scenery, and moods. Sheets of pure white snow cover the grays and browns of dormant plants in their beds, and glisten like satin jacquard on the blessed occasion of sun peeking out between blankets of clouds. I would be content to hibernate the season away, at home with my dogs and a good book or a dozen, yet it is also the best time of year to catch up with old friends and make some new ones.

Marty, my husband, was on the third day of his winter break from work and we were enjoying spending it together quietly with our three dogs. These dogs were our family; Toots, the nine year old glossy black Doberman/Labrador cross (a Dobrador, we called her) and the red and rust Dober-twins, year and a half old sister and brother, Sophie and Angus.

We were between snowstorms, and on this cold, inclement Friday we were feeling housebound and decided to break free by going to town to run some errands, do our grocery shopping, and mail bills. We loaded the dogs into the truck with the special 'dognapper' cab extension, and off we went in the Montana chill and the snow. We didn't have any idea of what was about to happen.

Suddenly, out of nowhere, I said, "Let's stop and say hi to Monica." My friend, Monica, is a dog groomer, a trainer, and a Doberman breeder. I had gotten my last beloved Dobie, Cosette, from her and I liked to visit with her occasionally and buy some dog treats in her shop. I would catch her up on how the Dober-twins were doing even though they came from another breeder. Marty and I had never gone by as a couple before. This wasn't Marty's "thing", listening to two avid dog lovers prattle on and on, but, for some reason beyond my understanding, this day I was inspired to ask, and he agreed to stop. Unusual...

When we approached Monica's place, we saw a huge, beat-up dinosaur of a motor home parked in her driveway. We pulled in beside it and noted the barking of a large and intimidating dog virtually vibrating the windows of the RV. As we entered the shop, Monica was listening to a disheveled woman talking loudly and emphatically about a small red Doberman she had at the end of a leash. She had a lot to say, and as she spoke, the little red waif whined and trembled uncontrollably.

The woman said she was sick of this animal, that it had bitten her. She had been on her way to the humane society to drop off the dog, whose name was "Lucky", when she stopped at Kmart. There happened to be a woman (coincidentally, my friend, Pam) walking a shelter dog outside the store in an effort to attract a family to adopt him. The woman asked directions to the shelter, saying she was headed there to drop off a dog. When Pam asked about the dog and learned it was a Doberman who had bitten her owner, she realized that the shelter would not be able to adopt out a biting Dobie; the liability would be too high, and the dog would most likely be euthanized.Without saying such, she suggested instead, that perhaps the woman should take her to Monica since she was a breeder and was better able to evaluate the situation and the dog. Perhaps she would know someone who was looking specifically for an adult Doberman to adopt. Besides, it was the middle of the winter, and the shelter was pretty crowded. So there she was, at Monica's to surrender Lucky. And there, by serendipity, we were also.

I listened to the woman speak of Lucky's history with a sense of horror. She claimed the dog was born in Toronto, Ontario, Canada, but that she had gotten her in Florida when the single man who owned Lucky didn't have time for her anymore. Even though this woman had her for two and a half years, she said Lucky had never bonded with her. She suspected the dog had never recovered from the loss of her previous owner. Lucky was now three and a half years old, wouldn't come when called, and would get loose and run away for several days at a time, coming back only when she was half starved and injured.

I saw an open wound on the dog's chest and asked about it. The woman said Lucky had run through a barbed wire fence five months before, and that she had taken her to the vet and had it stitched closed, but that Lucky had chewed the stitches out. So five months later there was still a partially healed wound that spanned the entire breadth of her chest. I detected no evidence of stitch marks.

The woman said she had a large male dog (the one we heard in the RV) who would bite Lucky's hind legs while she was eating to try to steal her kibble. The woman also said Lucky always slept on the bed, under the covers. There were no pedigree papers, but from what the former owner had told her she thought Lucky's birthday was probably May 10th. And, yes, she was spayed.

After telling her story the woman handed the leash over, said a quick farewell, and walked out the door. As the door slammed shut, Lucky leapt after her, exploding into a barking, crying, howling, door-climbing, and scratching fit. I'd never seen anyone surrender a dog before; I couldn't even imagine it. This poor little creature's life was now thrown into uncertainty. Who would want a Doberman who had bitten its owner? But if you had seen the woman, known the circumstances...

I sank to the floor in a flood of tears and gathered the trembling little girl into my arms. I looked at Marty pleadingly, but he said, "NO. We have three dogs, and that's enough." I was heartbroken but thought of my friend, Sally. She had rescued a Dobie once in Arizona and then another here in Montana several years ago. Now she had only one Black Labrador. She had also just lost her husband two months before and was grieving; perhaps she and Lucky could help each other heal.

I called Sally immediately and begged her to give this poor abandoned waif a chance. "Oh, Sally, she's so pretty! Wait until you see her face!" I exclaimed. She hesitantly agreed to take her but only on a trial basis. "I'll be there in an hour," I said.

Monica kept Lucky while we went home so I could return alone in my car. Lucky, huh? Why is it always the three-legged, one-eyed dog that gets saddled with that moniker? Well, if it hadn't worked for her so far, perhaps it could at least be prophetic.

I was surprised and impressed with Lucky for how willingly she came with me, how quickly she jumped into the Mustang. I talked to her during the whole twenty minute drive to Sally's house, telling her how beautiful I thought she was and how sorry I was that people can be so cruel. She took in all my words and my intent, even leaning across the console to give me a little kiss on the cheek with her soft pink rose petal tongue. A kiss of friendship. A kiss to comfort **me!** How could anyone surrender such a lovely little dog person? I could see there was a magnificent heart beating inside her chest. And I wanted her for my own. I wanted her *more than I've ever wanted anything* in my entire life. It was love at first sight. But we already had three...

Jeanie Notti- Fullerton

Chapter 2

Transition

When Lucky and I arrived at Sally's house, her young Black Labrador, Nikki, greeted Lucky with immense curiosity. Who was this strange red dog? Lucky was friendly and playful, posturing a game with her new companion. She was polite to Sally, sniffing her open hand and sitting when asked. It was dinnertime, and I knew she hadn't eaten yet. Sally found her a dish and fed her some good quality kibble. She ate well and then explored her new surroundings a little with Nikki close behind. Then Sally and I got serious about giving her a thorough once over.

The first thing that shocked us was how very tight her collar was. It was amazing she could even swallow. There were six dog tags on it, and she was apparently allergic to them because her neck and chest had no hair on them and were all broken out in a rash with oozing pustules. So off came the tags, and the nylon collar was loosened to a more comfortable notch. Her weight was okay, but the quality of her hair was very poor. It was so thin you could see her dry skin through it. She was bald on the top of her head from being chained under the motor home. She had old scars and fresh bite wounds. And her toenails were almost two inches long!! How could she walk, let alone run? She limped on one front foot and a hind leg. Yes, there were plenty of reasons for her persistent whimpering.

Enough! I couldn't bear to look for any more injuries. She was beautiful to me, and I repeated that I thought she was the prettiest little Doberman I'd ever seen. I was seeing her purely through the eyes of love.

I spent a couple of hours with Sally and the dogs, playing, hugging, and kissing Lucky, watching her figure it out. I hoped to have her good and tired so she would sleep well without suffering the anxiety of abandonment through the night. She knew all the commands I could think of: sit, stay, down, shake, fetch. She didn't need to be called to stay near me, it just seemed natural for her to want to be close.

Sally and I agreed that Lucky was a terrible name, and she wanted to change it to Jasmine--certainly a more feminine name for such a delicate girl. It may be a lot of change in a short period of time, but Lucky definitely needed a fresh start on many levels.

Having had years of experience using alternative and complementary medicines, especially homeopathy, in our family, I coached Sally on how to manage Jasmine's pain and treat her wounds until she could be seen by a vet.

I hugged the little red dog and kissed the top of her head and told her I would see her as soon as I could. As I drove away, the enormity of this experience suddenly hit me, and I burst into tears. I was horrified by the thought of what Lucky/Jasmine must have been through for the last three and a half years. And I was heartbroken that she wasn't coming home with me. It just didn't seem right that Providence brought her to my arms only to have us separated almost immediately.

For the next week I either called or went to see Jasmine and Sally every day. I could see this wasn't a match made in heaven. Sally was already stressed out and filled with grief and loss of her own. She found Jasmine's constant whining unnerving. And then one afternoon, Jasmine got away from her and went chasing deer across the neighbor's property, a crime she could have been shot for in Montana. She wouldn't answer to either of her names or to 'come', forcing Sally to chase after the little red criminal for a half hour. Jasmine insisted on sleeping on Sally's bed under the covers and then growled every time Nikki moved.

To make matters even more stressful, the woman who had surrendered Lucky found out from Monica where she was and drove her big old motor home out to Sally's house. Sally didn't know what to expect. Perhaps the woman's conscience was bothering her, but, as it turned out, she just wanted to drop off Lucky's dog dish and a couple of dog coats. Fortunately, Sally was able to dismiss her pretty quickly and without an emotional scene. The coats reeked so badly that Sally had to wash one of them five times, finally soaking it in fabric softener to kill the odor. But living in Montana with so little hair on her fragile body, Lucky/Jasmine needed the coats to survive any time she spent outside.

When I would visit, it was a joyous occasion. Jasmine would see me coming and greet me at the sliding glass doors with smiles, wiggling from her nose to her back toes. Then she would show off for me with all her tricks and antics, shaking hands, offering to play tug, posturing to Niki for a game. I found her to be beyond charming.

But by the end of the week, Sally was no longer so enamored of this complicated, whining, growling, and running dog. And Lucky/Jasmine had more medical problems than Sally was willing or able to deal with or spend the money to diagnose. The time had come...

Jeanie Notti- Fullerton

Chapter 3

Homecoming

Friday, January 3, 2003. 6:00 p.m. The phone rang. It was Sally. "I just can't deal with this dog anymore. I told you I'd take her on a trial basis, and I *did* try. But the fact is she bonded with you the instant you met. Every time she sees you she smiles and wiggles all over. She doesn't do that for me. You love each other. I'm leaving right now to bring her up to you. I'll be there in twenty minutes."

This was a dream come true! My heart soared! I had spent the entire week crying because Sally had **MY** dog, the one thing I wanted more than anything else, and I wanted her back! But what was I going to say to Marty? He had maintained his "No" stance all week.

He wasn't home, but he had the cell phone. I thought I'd better forewarn him. I dialed the cell number and held my breath until he answered. Then I blurted out, "So here's the deal. We can have a really big fight when you get home, or you can accept that we have another dog. And you have until you get home to decide." Then I hung up. After 30 years of marriage, he would know how serious I was. This was it. After a week of longing for her, I was ready, willing, and able to fight to the end for this charming dog I had been loving from afar.

The Providential Doberman

I was stomach-churning nervous about Sally's arrival however, concerned about how to introduce this newcomer to the other dogs. Toots wouldn't be a problem as she had become very accepting in her older years. There might be a problem with Angus, though, because we were awaiting the arrival of a veterinary surgeon in February to fix the torn anterior cruxiate ligament in his knee, and he wasn't supposed to get at all rambunctious.

What about Sophie? I had once heard that the worst dog fights were between the females. That wasn't Sophie's nature. She was the puppy who stepped up to the plate and offered to work to heal my broken heart when I first met her. Sophie the Healer... The one who loves people with handicaps of all sorts. She was just eleven months old when we took her to Bannack Days, a two day celebration of the old west, with reenactments, gold panning, cowboy poetry, and so much more. My Sophie spent the day seeking out people she could heal. Twice she pulled me to people in wheelchairs so she could lay her head in their laps and look up at them with all the intuitive understanding of a true healer as they stroked her silky head and absorbed her good energy. She touched those people's hearts to tears. Repeatedly Sophie sought out a teenaged girl with cerebral palsy until the girl had no choice but to fall madly in love with

25

her. Sophie would instinctively find the most broken heart in a crowd, and I was helpless to hold her back. She would pull until she choked in her determination to heal them. And so it was with her. Her energy was so beautiful, so perfect. Could she perform this kind of healing for another dog?

I'd keep Lucky/Jasmine on a leash until the introductions were made and we figured out how this was going to work. Whatever, it had to work because I didn't intend to *ever* say goodbye to her again.

When Sally arrived, I hugged her and thanked her for keeping Lucky/Jasmine for the week and for realizing this dog and I loved and needed each other. She handed me the dog dish, the clean coats, and the leash with Jasmine on the other end. My kindred dog smiled when she saw me. I smiled back at her and I was completely happy for the first time in a long while.

Then we walked into the house to three very curious dogs and their noses. Jasmine may have been the new girl in town, but she had attitude! She held herself very erect, alert as they all met and sniffed one another. Then she did the perfect thing; she went into a play stance! At first Sophie was a little hesitant as if she knew this new girl was fragile and tender. So they didn't get crazy, but when I unleashed Jasmine Sophie donned her tour guide demeanor to show her around her new home, focusing in on a favorite feature...the dog couch. Angus' size, one hundred pounds of muscle, bone, and sinew, was intimidating to Jasmine so she sent some low self-protective growls in his direction which he took very well, not aggressing, but backing off like the perfect gentleman I always believed him to be. He just stayed close to his mom.

It was dinner time for my dog children. I'm pretty sure it was the very first warm, homemade meal Jasmine had ever had. I hated to do this to her gastro-intestinal system, but I didn't have any commercial kibble. I'd been cooking for my dogs for years and this was how they ate: meat, vegetables, sprouted grains, essential fatty acid oils, and raw beef bones; real food. I decided to cut the ties with Jasmine's past starting immediately with the dog dish that she came with. The dish was as big as Angus, so he got her old stainless steel dish and she got his more appropriately sized stainless steel puppy dish.

I took Jasmine out to the laundry room where she could eat in peace without the others. When I set the heaping dish down for her she looked at me twice as if to say, "Is this for ME? All this???" before she dove in.She ate like a

27

typical Doberman, Too fast and with great enthusiasm. And when she finished, she licked her lips and looked at me as if she had won the gourmet dog food lottery! She had a glob stuck to the top of her nose so I whisked it off with my finger and let her lick it from my hand. I smiled as I felt her soft pink rose petal tongue.

After she ate I sat on the floor with Jasmine while we waited for Marty to arrive, and I talked to her about the importance of what was about to happen. "You don't have to convince me that you need to live with us. I lost my heart to you the instant I saw you. But you're going to have to convince the man who is going to be here in just a little bit that you need to stay. *Please* be as good as gold, and I know he'll see it. He's a good man and you're a very good dog."

When Marty walked through the back door, he was visibly upset. He didn't say a word as we all met him. He sat down to take his shoes off. Finally breaking the silence, I stated the crucial fact. "I don't think I could be in love with someone who couldn't open their heart wide enough to welcome in this dog."

It may sound like emotional blackmail, but it wasn't. I wasn't trying to get my way. In my mind there wasn't a 'my way' and 'his way'. There was just the **right** way. If he couldn't see the right thing to do was to stop the cycle of cruelty to this dog, to take the opportunity to change just one life for the better, then on what basis was there for a deep, meaningful relationship for the two of us? Especially when I saw it so clearly. Providence had spoken and we needed to listen.

At that very moment this sweet soul walked over, sat down directly in front of Marty, and offered him a fragile little paw. It was an offer of friendship from a gentle creature who had found it in her heart to forgive all of humanity for their cruelty. I was awestruck. It was exactly the right move at exactly the right moment. How could he resist? He accepted her handshake and began to pet her. My heart leapt...I could see she had broken his resolve.

We took our newest dog child into the living room where we could all begin to really get to know her. We decided to catalog her injuries so we could determine what we were dealing with on a medical level. We were especially concerned with the limp in her hind leg as we already had one dog scheduled for a fifteen hundred dollar knee surgery. I just hoped and prayed she didn't also have a torn anterior cruciate ligament or we would be in trouble.

Besides the things Sally and I found, the raw chest, the bald head, the hideously long toenails, the half-healed wound on her chest, and her poor hair coat, we found a broken and lifted toenail on her front left foot that exposed the quick with every step she took. Two of her toes on her front right foot had the tendons broken and instead of adorable Doberman "kitty paws" she looked like she had ostrich toes. Even after Sally had her toenails trimmed, they were disturbingly long. Her left rear knee had a huge bony knot on it where the knee cap was. We found several open bite wounds on her hind legs from the big Doberman she had lived with who bit her to get her food. There was a large open puncture wound low on the left side of her chest. Her belly was a mass of scars. There was an ugly puncture wound partially healed on the inside corner of her right eye. She had two broken teeth. There was a set of letters and numbers tattooed in her right ear. Her ears had been cropped, but no one had bothered to brace them, so they didn't stand; they simply winged out from the sides of her head. She was in pain, and she whimpered. I wept as we went from one end of her to the other while she patiently allowed us to examine her. There were twenty seven injuries all together in various stages of healing, besides the scars from old injuries.

She was certainly no breed standard beauty, with her short neck, straight top line, and low set tail. But she had a beauty of spirit that my eyes and heart saw over and above any physical appearance, any injury, any fault, any lack. "Feel her cheeks," I said to Marty. "It's like they are upholstered in pure satin." To stroke them was ecstasy to the touch.

Jasmine gave me one of those soft rose petal tongue kisses as I spoke gently to her. I returned her kiss and told her I would do my best to protect her from ever having this much pain again. I doctored the open wounds with natural medicines and gave her some Bach Rescue Remedy, some homeopathic arnica, and a couple of baby aspirin to ameliorate the pain and to help her sleep. My knowledge and interest in the healing arts and nutrition was going to be put to the test with this girl.

I could read in her beautiful dark golden topaz eyes that her life had been filled with sadness and that she was desirous of a gentle hand and loving arms to envelop her. At the same time there was a toughness, a street smart look of pure survival in those eyes. It was not just her body that had suffered, her psyche was badly damaged. There was emotional scar tissue on her heart and her mind that were far more serious than the visible injuries. I prayed with all my heart to be the person worthy of gaining her trust.

After our examination we let her be to explore and play with her new siblings. Sophie, Angus, and Toots were generous of spirit and were respectful of Jasmine's space. They were curious and undoubtedly concerned for me, but there was no indication of jealousy from them whatsoever. It was as if they innately understood we, all of us as a family, had just rescued this girl. It wasn't a project I was taking on all alone. We all had to agree to this, and our original three beloved dogs showed their agreement and support by their respect and distance when appropriate.

Jasmine had a large personal space around her when she was lying down, and she growled when the other dogs came too close. She was especially self-protective around Angus which was quite understandable after spending two and a half years being bitten by another dog much larger than she. She didn't know she had just met a true gentle giant of a Doberboy. When Jasmine would growl at him, he would avert his soft, liquidy brown eyes and back off. We praised him for his wisdom in knowing how to react. Only on her terms would she approach him and offer to play.

That first night with our new addition to the family was a typical 'winter in Montana' freezing cold night. The fire in the woodstove felt so warm and welcoming I decided to make a bed for us in front of it and sleep there with my precious new friend on her first night in her new home. Jasmine didn't particularly want to be cuddled, but it comforted her to be petted, so I gently stroked her little bald head, her satin face, and her fragile body until she went to sleep. She even cried in her sleep. It had been a difficult and painful three and a half year journey to my welcoming arms. And it had been a miserable week for me, as I had cried every day with longing for this little red waif who was supposed to be with me. The sadness of her past engulfed me, and as we laid there side by side together, I whispered, "Don't worry, sweet baby, the bad times are over now. You were dropped from heaven into my arms by an angel who loves dogs. We'll both be okay now. We'll find the joy, and no one will ever hurt you again. I love you so." I said a prayer of gratitude and softly wept myself to sleep beside her.

At three a.m. Marty came out to check on us and to feed the fire. He knew I had a difficult time sleeping on any hard surface, so he told me to go to bed, that he would stay with Jasmine for the rest of the night. I hesitated, not wanting to leave her for even a moment. But I knew

I had to work on this particular Saturday and needed to feel rested. I also needed to allow her new dad to comfort her so he would bond as tightly as I already had. I agreed to let him stay with her for the rest of the night. She was a waif no longer...

Chapter 4

A New Life isDawning

Jasmine slept as well as could be expected in a new environment. When she woke up in the morning, she knew she had landed in a good place. She bid me good morning with such happy smiles! And she was ready to play a quick 'tough and tumble' game with Sophie before breakfast. On Saturdays the dad made pancakes for everyone, so she was immediately part of a family tradition. Everyone sat pretty for their pieces of the hotcakes. Jasmine was a little bit too enthusiastic...we'd have to work on "easy" so we didn't end up with missing fingers! Amazingly, there was no aggression, no growling, no jealousy, no posturing for dominance. The three long term residents realized there was another dog person who was to be shared with and they accepted that with generosity and grace. It was much like the mercy we show in human society when we see someone in need and are willing to lend them a helping hand in whatever way we can. My dogs were being kind and compassionate and I was never more proud or more in love with them than at that moment.

We have a dog door into a large, secure dog yard that they could access at any time they needed to go out to potty, and Sophie was quick to show Jasmine the outside. Otherwise I took her outdoors on a leash only, knowing she had been a runner. It was my goal to keep her safe, not to have a neighbor shoot a chasing dog.

Her collar was terrible for her. It was a nice, even a fancy, nylon collar. But Jasmine's skin was so bare, so raw, and so thin that the edges of the nylon just seemed too harsh. I quickly cut and sewed a strip of soft black polar fleece to cover it until she healed and until we could buy a new leather collar--one with a brass identification plate on it,*not* tags. Nothing to irritate her any longer. And before there could be a new collar with a brass name tag, we had to find a new name...

Lucky...well, not until now. Jasmine...no explanation, it just didn't work. She didn't want to answer to either of those names. She didn't come when called by them. It was as if she didn't even hear them. Odd, since she knew plenty of typical dog commands. She responded to sit, lie down, shake, fetch...but not her own name. Nor did she seem to know "come." The one command that could protect her from danger she didn't respond to.

Dobermans are a strong-minded, strong-willed breed. Their intelligence is legendary. They are also the most loyal, devoted dogs imaginable. As military dogs, they were called "Velcro dogs" because of their willingness to stick devotedly to their partner through thin and thick, even at the cost of their own lives. For this Doberman not to have bonded with her owner says a great deal about the owner, not the dog. And not to acknowledge her own name...bizarre.

Until I could think of something better, I would call her Jazz. My head swirled with possible names for her, but I decided to let her choose her own. She was smart, and I would know when the correct name resonated with her. She'd let me know. I would just throw out names and see what happened. It could take some time, but a new name was too important to rush into. Especially in her case.

Chapter 5

To Slay a Dragon

Life had taken a big U-turn for Jazz, and that meant there was great potential for insecurity and confusion for her. But there would be no more abandonment. This was forever. I felt it was necessary to keep her by my side for awhile to help her understand and feel assured that she really was mine now. Besides, her new dad had plans for that Saturday morning, and it was too soon to leave her at home alone with the other dogs. That meant she would be going to work with me on this wintry day.

At that time I worked at a historical house museum, and even during my winter layoff, I occasionally agreed to go in and give a special tour. This day I was opening the house for a luncheon along with a special tour for a woman's group. Now, how was that going to work with a dog in tow? I had actually done a tour with a dog once before...my beloved Cosette, when we were evacuated from our home during a bad fire season. It worked out fine. It was like having a service dog with us. At that time there were no rules against it. But I didn't know how this girl would act. So I called my teenage volunteer, Trista, and asked for her assistance. I asked if she would follow along on the tour with Jazz, my new dog, so Jazz could see me at all times and not feel separated. If she fussed, Trista could take her out and just stay with her.

I bundled up Jazz in the red quilted coat that came with her although she let me know she didn't like it by not being very cooperative in putting it on...note to self...make a new fleece coat for her later. Then I loaded her in the car, and away we went to pick up Trista and do our duties to historical preservation. Jazz greeted Trista warmly and Tristawas immediately in love with her.

The ladies on the tour were equally as charmed by Jazz's friendliness. Most of her injuries were covered by the little red quilted coat and the fleece collar cover, so their focus was on her personality, not her pain. She often whimpered and whined, but Trista petted her the entire time, and there were moments when I could touch her and reassure her that all was well. I told her we were just on an adventure--the first of many.

About half-way through the tour, Jazz became inconsolable though, and dragged Trista to the front of the crowd so she could be next to me. At that point I explained the seriousness of her situation to my group. One poor lady gasped and threw her hands over her mouth at the thought of this sweet soul being mistreated. When Jazz heard her she pulled Trista to the woman and this kindly little dog began to comfort the woman with nuzzles and licks, as if to say, "It's okay,

I'm going to be happy from now on with my new mom."
We were all misty-eyed for the rest of the tour.

After the tour, while the ladies were enjoying a catered lunch, the caterer brought Trista and I each a plate of Pistachio Encrusted Chicken Salad and crusty bread. We shamelessly shared it with Jazz, and mused at how she went from being chained under a beat-up motor home to touring a mansion and having a catered lunch from a five-star restaurant in such a short period of time.

Just as the ladies finished their lunch and the caterer was completing his clean up, I got a phone call from Marty.

"The woman who gave the dog away was just here. She wants her dog back, and she is heading down there to get her."

I was livid!!! I burst into tears and asked him how this happened. Apparently the woman had called Sally and when she told her she no longer had the dog, that the dog was now with me, the woman became angry that Lucky was being "shuffled around." She asked Sally where we lived and went straight to our house. When Lucky wasn't there, she irately demanded to know where I was with her, and Marty told her. Now she was on her way to my workplace and would be there in just a few minutes! I was furious! All I could do was hang up on him. Why didn't he just tell her she had no rights to the dog anymore, that Lucky/Jasmine was our dog now? I knew I'd have to deal with that later. Right then I had to face down a dragon.

No sooner had I locked up the house than sure enough, the woman pulled up into the public parking lot in the monstrosity of a motor home. Jazz, Trista, and I drove out to meet her. I was grateful all my tourists were gone. If I had to take this matter to fisticuffs, if I had to call the law, whatever I had to do, I was prepared to fight for this sweet dog;**MY dog**.

As we pulled up in the lot, the ratty door on the motor home slowly opened. The woman climbed out, pushing bags and loose garbage back in as she did. You could see trash stacked high through the huge windshield. The striped awning was torn and drooping because its bracket was broken and the whole tangle was hanging half off the side of the RV. And inside you could hear the big male Doberman barking loudly.

We got out of the Mustang. I asked Trista to stay with us, and if things got heated and I needed her to, I would have her take Jazz back to the car. As the brawny woman aggressively strode toward us I noticed she was dressed in the same dirty gray-green sweater and worn jeans she had on when I last saw her a week ago, only they were another week dirtier this time. She smelled acrid and musty even in the open winter air.

When she neared us the woman blurted out, "Lucky!" There was no softness in her voice, it was harsh and commanding. I let Jazz have the length of the leash to see what she would do. She went ahead tentatively and cautiously. Then she reached out and gave the woman's hand a little nudge with her nose. Immediately after this encounter Jazz turned away from her and came back to stand by my side. There was no warm fuzzy greeting between the two of them, simply a brief acknowledgement by the dog that the woman was there. I reached down and put my hand on Jazz's satin cheek.

The woman took a combative stance with her hands on her hips and a crazed look in her eyes. Then she loudly demanded she be given "her" dog back. I became so angry I could feel my face redden with heat and the tears hanging on the edges of my eyelids.

As calmly as I could, I said, "You surrendered this dog a week ago. You didn't care what happened to her then. Why do you want her back now?"

"My other dog misses her."

"What does he miss? Does he miss beating up on her? You let him get away with biting her legs and eating her food!! Do you miss that?"

"That's not how it was!"

"You told us yourself that was what accounted for the wounds on her back legs. And how do you explain all the other injuries she has? Like the broken toes and the terrible limp in her hind leg?"

"She never had a limp while I had her!"

I turned to Trista and asked her to walk Lucky around so the woman could see. As she walked away I passionately exclaimed, "Look at her limp! That isn't new. That's an old injury. We catalogued all her injuries last night. There are *twenty-seven* of them! All old and only partially healed. And that doesn't count all the old scars! She's in constant pain, and then you added to her emotional pain by rejecting her! I stepped up to the plate to find her a safe, permanent home and the best home for her ended up being MINE!! If you can't accept that perhaps we should call the sheriff's office and have an officer come and decide whose dog this really is!"

I saw the woman's fists clench and her jaw tighten. But she backed down. "I don't want to call the sheriff. I just want my dog back!"

Looking her straight in the eye I said, "Can't you see she isn't your dog anymore? She doesn't want to be with you! *You surrendered her!* You said you couldn't stand her!"

"But I've changed my mind! Now I miss her! And my other dog misses her!"

"We aren't getting anywhere with this. I'll tell you what we'll do. We'll end this thing where it began. I'll meet you at Monica's and we'll let *her* decide whose dog this is now. Will that settle your mind?"

"Yes."

"I'll meet you there in twenty minutes, after I take my assistant home."

Meanwhile Jazz had literally dragged Trista back to my car. Trista could see she was terrified and confused by this confrontation. So they got in the car where Jazz could feel warm and safe from her former keeper. When I got in they were cozied up together in the front seat where Trista had her wrapped tightly in her arms and was comforting the trembling Jazz.

I was apoplectic with rage. How could this woman even THINK of approaching me about getting this dog back? Like I wasn't there when she gave her up! Like I didn't have eyes to see the abuse the dog had suffered! I wanted to turn her in to the sheriff's office and see if they'd confiscate her other dog too! But I knew the law on these things. She housed the dog and he had food and water, so it wouldn't matter what I thought was wrong about the situation, that was what the law would see and he'd remain. This dog, **MY dog**, was another matter. She gave her up, and I had witnesses to it. I called Monica to give her a heads up about what was going on.

I cried and ranted and shook all the way to Trista's house. I felt bad that she had to be a witness to this kind of drama. She didn't sign on for this as part of her volunteer experience! But she was a comfort to Jazz in a crisis and I appreciated her for it. I told her I'd call when it was all over and let her know what happened.

On the way back into town I tried to explain what was going on to little Lucky/Jazz who was sitting in the passenger seat trembling with fear and with a glazed look in her eye. She was far too stressed to be reassured at that moment. I collected myself and my emotions just as I drove into Monica's driveway. Once again I prepared myself to go toe to toe with a dragon. I looked Jazz in the eyes and smiled at her. Then I gave her a kiss on the forehead to give us strength.

As Jazz and I walked in, I could tell the woman was filling Monica's ear with ravings about how this was her dog and she didn't want Lucky shuffled from home to home so she had come back to reclaim her.

I greeted Monica and then asked her to watch the dog walk. The limp was obvious. It was painful to see. I told her we had counted her injuries. And I told her that Marty and I had committed to keeping this dog. All the while **MY dog** clung tightly to my side, staring at me with love eyes and nuzzling my hand. She did not attempt to greet her former owner a second time.

Suddenly the woman burst out yelling, "What have you done to my dog?? It's like she doesn't even know me anymore! *Lucky, come here!*"

The little dog didn't even acknowledge her. At that moment I understood. Those words, her name, coming from this woman's mouth were like acid being thrown in her face. I wouldn't have responded either.

Coolly, I said, "Do we need to call the sheriff to decide this, or are you going to let Monica make the decision as to whose dog she believes this to be?"

The enraged woman looked at Monica and said, "Well? Whose dog is she?!"

Monica said, "It's obvious to me that the dog loves Jeanie, and Jeanie loves the dog. You should be grateful. This dog could not have landed in a better home, and I will vouch for that. The dog belongs to her."

Through my tears I vehemently added, "And this WILL be the end of the matter. I don't want you contacting me again to salve your guilty conscience about this dog."

With that the woman once again walked out the door and slammed it behind her. This time however, the dynamics were completely different. There was no reaction from Jazz. She just kept looking at me with faith that she was now with someone who would keep her safe. Her heart had forgiven the woman and had

49

moved on. I went to my knees and gave her a big hug. "Let's go to **our** home," I said to her. I hugged Monica, thanked her, and **MY dog** and I went to the car.

When we got home I expressed myself adamantly about what I thought of Marty allowing the woman to come down to my work to reclaim "Lucky". I felt it was feeding me to a dragon to allow that to happen. With that I realized that there was a serious problem we would have to deal with at some point in our marriage. I had never felt truly safe in all my life. I'd surrounded myself with dogs whose reputation is to defend and protect their owner if it meant their death, because I didn't feel safe or protected even with those who loved me. I needed him to help me feel less vulnerable, not more so. How would we ever reconcile this? I couldn't deal with all of this right then. It was too much. I felt like I had been beaten and then dipped in acid and then punched in the stomach. As Scarlett O'Hara would say, "I'll think about it tomorrow. Tomorrow is another day."

Chapter 6

Cleansing Away The Past

The next day, Sunday, you could see the adjustments were happening quickly. We were taking longer walks to show Jazz the perimeters of her new homeland. She was curious about everything. And Sophie was fascinated by her. Jazz was a willing playmate for her, showing submissive behavior, allowing Sophie to put her mouth around her head (playing lion tamer, we called it) and boxing with her sportingly. She set boundaries with Angus that he tolerated. We gave him some extra attention to ameliorate any tension he was feeling from it.

"Bellasera? How about Bellasera? Sera?"Nope...

After two nights I decided I couldn't sleep on the floor anymore with Jazz though. And I wasn't going to let her into my bed unless she had a bath. She didn't smell bad nor did she have any skin conditions or parasites, but for the pure principle, she needed a bath. And when I bathe one, I bathe them all. Sophie hates baths, so I wasn't going to do her first and give Jazz a bad impression. Finally I just decided to take the plunge and bathe my new kid first.

"Come on, Eliza Doolittle. What do you think of Eliza?" No...

I leashed her and led her into the bathroom. When I asked her to jump into the tub, she clearly did not know what it was all about. So finally I lifted her in. That was a big leap of faith for her. I stripped down to my underwear and sat on the edge of the tub with my feet inside it. I took the hand held shower and adjusted the water to just the right warmth while holding onto the leash the entire time not knowing what she would do. I first got her toes wet, along with my own. Then I worked up her body and across her back and down her chewed up hind legs until she was all wet. I could tell this was a new experience for her. People often think short-haired dogs don't need to be bathed, but they enjoy being clean and groomed just like the long-haired breeds do. Dobermans tend to have oily skin and their coats look better when shampooed occasionally.

I used a special bar of expensive natural dog soap to work up a nice lather all over her. She relaxed and enjoyed the feeling of the slippery soap as it slid smoothly across her skin. I massaged the lather in circles from one end of her to the other and down each delicate leg and across her tummy and gently up her sore chest and neck. The tea tree oil in the soap would help cleanse the injuries. I rinsed her and because she seemed to like this thing called a bath I put a natural conditioner on her and massaged that in for a few minutes. I let it sit on her skin while I took a washcloth and the bar soap and gently washed her pretty face with the satin cheeks. I gingerly washed in each ear, careful not to go too deep but cleaning the nooks and crannies. Then I got out a toothbrush and the chicken flavored toothpaste, and she learned what it was to have her teeth brushed. Finally, one last long warm rinse. She had very clearly enjoyed this experience. I turned the water off and grabbed a towel. As soon as I got the first of the water blotted off of her, she gave a good shake and jumped out of the tub.

I don't know what it is about a bath, but it always makes my dogs go goofy. Jazz nearly exploded out of the bathroom, her rear end tucked under and trying to pass her front end. She raced down the hallway with such glee! We laughed as she grinned and twirled and ran through the house, stopping to shake every twenty seconds or so. Thankfully she actually liked having a bath...maybe Sophie would take a hint? By the time I got all four dogs bathed, the house was a dripping mess of wet footprints and sprayed shakes. But everyone was treated equally. No one was left out. And that is how it would always be.

Titian is an artist's shade of red... "How about Titia?Titia is a pretty name! What do you think?" Nope.

The bath left Jazz looking a great deal better and smelling sweet and fresh. Unused to this kind of attention to personal hygiene, you could see that her self-esteem had just launched into outer space. She now smelled like everyone else in the family and that is important to dogs, whose olfactory sense is so much more acute than ours. We now all smelled like we belonged together. Like a family.

"Sienna! Ooh, I like that name! C'mon Sienna! Sienna! ... Sienna?" Not even...

Our third night of holistic eating and so far Jazz had no gastro-intestinal upset associated with the switch over. She was immediately crazy about her new mom's cooking and as I gathered the dishes up to fix dinner, she became restless and began pacing and whining and even barking and sort of yodeling at about one hundred twenty ear-piercing decibels. And it was non-stop. It took me a few minutes to get their dishes prepared because I also add the supplements they need to stay healthy just before serving it. And each dog had a different regimen, depending on what was going on at the time, so making dinner was much more of a production than pouring some dry dog food in a dish.

Apparently this was too much for my impatient little friend, and she thought nagging me might hurry the process. Her eagerness was unfortunately contagious, making the Dober-twins restless, too. Pretty soon Sophie was whining and pacing, and Angus was drooling all over his legs, his chest and the floor. My once quiet and mannerly Twins were infected with a new enthusiasm for dinnertime. By the time I began placing the dishes down for them, Jazz was spinning circles and jumping and yipping like crazy. We would work on getting a grip on that after she had settled in. For then I took it as a compliment.

"Here's your dinner, Caramia. C'mon, Cara. Cara, sit. Mia, sit. Sit, Mia. Okay, just sit. Good girl. Thank you, Anonymous."

That night we moved from the floor in front of the fire into my bed with the clean, fluffy flannel sheets and the puffy comforter. Very quickly Jazz taught me that she was used to sleeping under the covers at the foot of the bed. That was okay. Sophie slept higher up in the bed. Angus and Toots both had beds on the floor, though Angus always joined me for cuddles after the dad got up at five a.m. to go to work. It was comfortable for the two of us to have Sophie in bed with us, but this little newcomer made for a very crowded double bed!

However it was warm and cozy--I could foresee many three dog nights ahead.

"Let's go to bed, Angelica. Angelica? Angel?" Absolutely not.

What I didn't foresee was that Jazz had very real issues about the bed. Sally told me she growled every time Niki moved. But her issues were bigger than that. Where she would tolerate Sophie on the bed with her, she went ballistic when Angus even came near the bed. After some observation and meditation on the matter, we realized that dinner time wasn't the only time she was attacked by the other dog she had lived with. It was obvious that being under the blankets made her feel safe until she perceived someone was going to jump on her.

Her growls were not low warning growls but instead were loud, vicious and aggressive, with dilated pupils and flying saliva. And she let loose with them every time Angus moved. Jazz had uncanny hearing when it came to the boy's every step, stretch, yawn, and blink, and she would adjust her growl to threaten him accordingly. Several times during the night, we were startled awake, to put it mildly, by her vocal explosions. She never made a peep over being nudged or disturbed by our movements or by our feet, but in her way of thinking Angus was someone to be concerned about.

Angus is as smart, sensitive, and gentle as he is magnificent to look at. I had great confidence that he'd learn to work around Jazz's behavior. We would all have to make adjustments to deal with someone this complicated. But we were blessed with large generous hearts, and we'd figure this out...

Chapter 7

Learning Trust and Building Faith

Early the next morning, Monday, I took Jazz out on leash as I had been doing. She was giddy with happiness. We were developing a great relationship. She seemed to like my voice and listened when I spoke, though she still wouldn't acknowledge a name. We were still a bit name challenged.

"How about Taylor, like in Liz Taylor? No? ...Oh, right, wrong eye color."

I hated putting the awful collar on Jazz, even with the fleece cover, and I tended to keep it loose. I gave her a long leash so she and Sophie could explore and romp a little when suddenly, in a split second of play, she slipped her collar. Oh, no. She refused to come. She took off trotting around the five acres with her nose down. I followed her all over, in the front field, then the north field. She would turn and look me directly in the eyes every few seconds, but she would not come. The other dogs could see this wasn't a good thing and stayed close to me. Then she went under the fence onto one of our neighbor's property. I was panicked. If she caught a scent and ran, I'd be just sick. But she continued to stop and look me in the eyes.

Suddenly I realized Jazz wasn't running away. She was exploring. The looks were a reassurance from her. I needed to learn to trust her, to have faith that she had bonded as deeply with me as I had with her. I stopped following her, and I took the other dogs and went in the house. Then I sat and prayed that I was right. I kept track of her by watching her through the windows. She was never out of my sight. Then within five minutes (a very long five minutes) there was a whine at the back door. When I opened the door she ran in, smiling, and we had what amounted to a glorious reunion celebration, with hugs and kisses and lots of cookies! She ran around her home with a certainty that this was where she *wanted* to be. My faith in her was fulfilled and she could now be outside with supervision but without a leash.

At 8:30 I called to make an appointment for a vet check for Jazz. I thought I had better talk directly to my veterinarian, Dr. Hans Boer, since we had been through some really interesting and occasionally frightening times together with my dogs. And this may be one of the more interesting.

I had first met Dr. Hans when my Cosette was a puppy. A gorgeous black and rust Doberman puppy I had chosen (or rather, who had chosen me) from Monica's first Dobie litter when she was three days old. I visited her every week until she could come home with me at six and a half weeks. She was my "empty nest" puppy. I had gotten her to help fill the hole in my soul after our son, Benj, left home, and got married. I no longer felt like a mom, a role I cherished. I needed a baby of some sort to help me through. Someone who needed me.Cosette filled that role beautifully. To look at her was to see my heart walking outside my body.

Hans had just moved to the Bitterroot Valley and opened a practice across the street from Marty's aunt and uncle. My vet, Dr. Laurie Kelly, had retired, so the timing was good. We didn't know at our initial meeting what lay ahead for my beautiful puppy/baby. At eight weeks old Cosette was diagnosed with severe von Willebrand's disease, her blood was missing the clotting factor that allows the platelets to stick together to make a viable clot. She was a 'bleeder.' It stood in the way of a relaxed life for us, because even a bad bruise could be life threatening for Zette. As a very wise veterinarian friend of mine, Dr. Bob Brophy said, "You need to treat her like the royalty of Russia." So I was hyper-vigilant with my precious girl. I carried a specialized first aid kit with us everywhere, which included alternative clotting agents such as the herbal Yunnan Paiyao and the homeopathic remedies phosphorus and arnica.

Later Cosette was diagnosed with hypothyroidism and then, a year after that, congestive heart failure. Our veterinarian/chiropractor, Dr. Patti Prato, said she thought Zette may have incompletely formed kidneys, as she was incontinent along with her other maladies. She was just the unfortunate throwback to many generations of Doberman genetics. There is hardly any disease these incredible animals don't have in their genes somewhere, and Cosette seemed to inherit more than her share. She died at four and a half years old from the heart condition.

When she died, I wanted to go with her. I had spent her entire life loving her with my whole heart, taking her everywhere, learning everything I could about alternative health care and holistic diets so I could fight to give her the best quality life she could possibly have. And all she could stay was four and a half years. Hans and I had fought a fine fight together to keep her alive and happy. When it was over, I could hardly go on. The grief was unbearable. Marty said we needed to get another puppy as soon as possible to fill my empty arms.

Two months later came Sophie. She was holistically raised, and I was determined to make no mistakes with her whatsoever. She tested von Willebrand's disease clear and had no heart disease in her background. We did an alternative method of vaccination with her, single antigens alternating, to protect her from Parvovirus and distemper.

Just one and a half weeks after Sophie's first birthday, she was diagnosed with Parvovirus…vaccine failure. It developed into one of the worst cases Hans had ever seen. I had faith in him to do his best. He worked hard to keep her alive after she collapsed thirty six hours later. Marty and I spent the night at Hans' veterinary clinic with her, and it was a good thing we did. She was too weak to stand to vomit and would most likely have aspirated (inhaled her own vomit) and died had Marty not held her upside down, allowing gravity to help clear her stomach. She was released only because I took a week off work to stay with her every second, changing her IV solution bags, and taking her in daily for an antibiotic shot. Sophie's survival was finally assured on September 8th, 2002, the one year anniversary of Cosette's death.

Just two and a half months later Sophie's brother, Angus, was diagnosed with a torn anterior cruxiate ligament in his knee, and we were waiting for the specialist surgeon to cycle around in February to do the surgery. Because he was a young, large-bodied dog with poorly shaped knees, we were having an expensive TPLO (Tibial Plateau Leveling Osteotomy) surgery done on him to redesign the lower leg bone (the tibia), so the upper bone (the femur) would have a place to "park". We were investing considerably in Dr. Hans' children's college fund! I knew before I called what he was going to say about me acquiring one more mouth to holistically feed...

"Jeanie, you don't need another dog right now."

"Somehow I knew you were going to say that, but wait until you meet her. Trust me, Hans, she was meant to be **MY** dog."

He occasionally does complimentary vet checks for our local humane association, so he took mercy on me, and agreed to do a free basic check on Jazz. I would pay for any extras like x-rays on her hind legs. We made the appointment for Friday morning. I could manage her pain with my own remedies until then. I had to have faith that she would be given a clean bill of health...

Jeanie Notti- Fullerton

Chapter 8

One Final Hurdle

Marty and I both agreed there was only one thing that could break this deal. We had a ten month old grandson, Caleb, whose name means "dog" in Hebrew. Jazz had to be good with children.

I was looking forward to babysitting Caleb that Monday morning while his Mom had an appointment. If Jazz showed not to be trustworthy with children, we were in trouble. I couldn't even bear to think of what that would mean. I had to have faith it would all be fine. I called our daughter-in-law, Molly, who is a very relaxed, balanced Mom, and told her all about Jazz in advance. Then I sat down to have yet another talk with my precious new dog child about what was about to happen and what was expected of her. She stared me straight in the eyes, focused on every word I said.

"Please, *please*, *PLEASE*, Jazz, you have just one more hurdle to cross. You have to be good with this baby. You have to…you just *have to*."

I was nervous, with a touch of anticipatory nausea. And not enough sleep, so the anxiety was that much worse. When Molly arrived, she brought Caleb in with all the paraphernalia that goes with a baby. We sat down on the big leather couch to make the introductions. Jazz and Sophie were right there poking their noses in the baby's face and wiggling all over. We immediately knew Jazz liked children. She sat down in front of Molly and shook hands with her and charmed her as she had all the other people she had met. With a clean, shiny, and sweet smelling body her injuries didn't seem so off-putting. After meeting Jazz, it was easy for Molly to leave her beautiful baby Caleb-whose-name-means-dog with his protective Nan and her four large dogs. My relief was indescribable, and when Molly left I called Marty right away with tears of joy falling off my lashes and told him the good news.

That morning I learned something wonderful.

Caleb was crawling very well and we spent most of our time down on the floor, moving, playing with blocks, stacking plastic donuts, and laughing. Sophie and Jazz were right in the middle of the action. Angus took a post on the hide-a-bed/dog couch, up above it all as this big, brave Dober-boy found the little active human boy somewhat intimidating. Unimpressed with it all, Toots found a quiet corner where she could take a nap. When it came time to change Caleb's diaper I had two very eager helpers at my side, offering their built in baby wipes, squeezing in to lick his toes and legs while I took care of the more delicate areas. He giggled and kicked and squealed and squirmed over the whole thing, which just got them more excited to take care of him. Their maternal switches were flipped. They doted on him. Nanny dogs!

"How aboutNanny? Wasn't that the dog in Peter Pan?" Ooh... **big** no...

I admittedly got a little tired of the competition. Our house is very small, twelve hundred square feet, and four big dogs fill the space completely. I decided to make more crawling room for Caleb by putting up the baby gates and blocking the dogs out of the living room. Then he could move freely without a nanny dog in his face or nudging his little round butt and tipping him over on his nose.

All was well for about two minutes. The dogs were all lined up next to the hallway baby gate when Jazz began to whine. It built to a crescendo. I walked across the room to get a baby toy, and when I looked back Caleb had crawled over to the baby gate. He was sitting with his tiny hand reaching through, touching Jazz, and they were both crying as though the Berlin Wall had just been erected between long lost lovers. This would never do...down came the baby gate, and there was nothing but licks and giggles for the next few minutes until they got over the separation.

The Providential Doberman

That was when I realized something so wonderful it took my breath away. Inside that tiny little boy beat a heart like mine, the tender heart of a true animal lover. My heart soared with love for Caleb-whose-name-means-dog, and these adoring creatures I have been blessed to share my home and my life with.

I had a second thought, though, about what that would mean for him if he stayed a tender-heart. For those of us who are soft and open to falling in love with the creatures we share our planet with our road is not easy. We experience incredible joys and great laughter. But there is another side to it...the deep sorrow of loss. Caleb just exhibited both on a smaller plane. I became profoundly aware that if he continued to be tender I would have to help him to understand somehow that the love and joy were worth the pain at the end. Until then we would just bask in the pleasure of each day spent loving these animals.

Because of the noise they made while showing off for him, he would call our dogs "The Grrr's", for the next year until he could say each name. And we would hope to have a name for the new girl by then...

71

Jeanie Notti- Fullerton

Chapter 9

Miles of Smiles

I had to run errands in town Wednesday afternoon, and, in a fit of bravery, I decided to leave Jazz with her dad for the first time. He had gotten the dogs big beef knuckle bones at the local butcher shop, and everyone was set with a bone to chew while I was gone. I was still nervous about leaving Jazz, having become somewhat over-protective of her. Dads tend to be a lot more relaxed about things when they are left in charge. Less observant. My thoughts were flying… 'What if she gets hurt? What if there is a fight? What if she sees me go and has a big meltdown? What if Marty names her something awful like Diesel while I'm gone?! Sooner or later I'll have to leave her home with him, and, as frightening as that thought is, it may as well be sooner.' I held my breath and drove away.

I did my errands at breakneck velocity, exceeding the speed limits, racing through the grocery store, practically jumping the turnstile at the post office. I stopped short of being rude, pushing in front of elderly people in line, or running over pedestrians, but I didn't have time to be my usual friendly self, either. Then I rushed back home eager to see how things had gone.

As I drove up the driveway, there were no dogs in sight. I held my breath for a second time. When I parked my car and turned the engine off, Marty opened the back door and out came a thundering herd of dogs! At the head of the pack, was the new little red princess, wiggling and grinning like I'd been gone a month instead of an hour.

"Hi, everyone! And look at you, my little Smiley-Miley girl!"

At that moment she stopped and the look on her face changed completely. Her eyes got big and round. It was a dawning of recognition. A response to what I just said like none she'd ever had before. It was as if a light had just been flipped on in a pitch black room. And what she suddenly saw in the brightness of that light was a treasure. I paused.

"Is that it? Is it Miley?"

She began twirling and smiling and when I leaned over to her she jumped up and gave me a rose petal tongue kiss on the cheek as if to say, "Finally!! Finally a name I like!"

"Okay, sweetheart, there you have it! Miley it is!"

It was an accident, a play on words in a moment of pure delight. But it was a happy sounding name said in the joy of seeing her come to me, and it was the name SHE chose, not one forced on her. Her new name tasted as sweet as honey, and it was safe in our mouths. From that moment on, she listened for her name or any nickname that was a derivative thereof: Miles, My-My, etc. It was important to her. A treasure. It was as beautiful to her as she was to me. She came when she was called, and she never ignored a request of her again. Well, almost never again...

Chapter 10

The Vet Check

Friday morning -- the day I had been eagerly anticipating, but not without trepidation. My hope was for Hans to be able to answer many of my questions during this check-up. Miley had suffered for a long while and I longed to find all the sources of her misery and heal them once and for all time.

When we got to the clinic, I introduced Miley to everyone, but she wasn't her usual charming self. She was anxious. She didn't want to be there. She was nervous and whiny and wanted to pull me back out the door. I imagined she had not always had good experiences at vet clinics. Even so, once Dr. Hans came in she was cooperative and stoic, as is the Doberman way.

Hans did all the typical check-up things; she weighed in at sixty-five pounds, a good weight for her. Her fecal test showed she was free of parasites. Temperature normal, eyes clear, heart and lungs sounded good. Then he looked at all the injuries. (We later learned from transferred medical records that the woman lied to us-- she did not have the long cut on her chest stitched shut, she opted to let it heal on its own because of cost). When he got to Miley's ears, he gave me bad news. Her tiny ears were full of needle-like shards of cheatgrass, a brittle, seedy, noxious dry-land grass. She would have to be anesthetized to get it all out. And that would be a good time to x-ray her hip and knee. He allowed me to stay with her every second.

There were six pieces of cheatgrass in one ear and seven in the other. None of it had damaged her eardrums, amazingly. After Hans removed the grass shards, Deana, the vet tech, clipped her too-long toenails. This was the second time in a week they had been clipped. They had deformed her feet. The x-rays of the hip and knee did not show anything particularly wrong with them. He tested her to see if she had a torn anterior cruxiate ligament and found no sign of that being the problem. There seemed to be no clinical explanation for the hind leg limp. All the rest of her troubles were things that time and care and love would relieve. Things I was good at.

When Hans was done with Miley, I sat with her on a blanket on the floor of the surgery waiting for her to awaken. I gave her some homeopathic remedies to make the transition out of the anesthetic easier for her. As I was waiting, I was stroking her and looking closely at all the scars and wounds. With her asleep I noticed something I hadn't seen before. I commented to Hans on the really big spay scar she had. Hans looked up from what he was doing and said, "Jeanie, that isn't a spay scar, that's a Caesarean scar."

79

I gasped. This was just too much. Not only was she obviously a product of backyard breeding, but she should never have been allowed to have puppies! I was horrified. I could have screamed. She had been in the hands of irresponsible people from her conception on. It's just infuriating to see what this kind of treatment does to a dog. Miley had never been cherished. She was a commodity. Used and abused and thrown away when no longer convenient. I was so angry with the world, so furious I couldn't speak. All I could do was weep for her and for every dog like her.

"She has a good home now," Hans said.

"Yeah. The bad days are over," I said softly to her.
I called Marty as soon as Miley was awake and told him the news. There was much to be relieved about. The best part was that she did not have a torn cruxiate ligament. She would not have to undergo any major surgery to experience a full recovery. Dr. Hans had no clinical explanation for the limp, though. The next stop would be our friend in Missoula, Dr. Patti Prato, who is a veterinary chiropractor and acupuncturist. Understanding Miley's need for energetic balancing, I had already made an appointment for her for the next week...

Chapter 11

Let's Do Lunch and Go Shopping

Following Miley's good vet check and given her clean bill of health, I figured it was time for us to celebrate by having our first Girlfriend Lunch, an occasion I instituted with Cosette. So off we went to McDonald's where we each got a cheeseburger--no pickles, no onions. We parked by the picnic area so we could watch the squirrels, and I meted out bites, knowing that, given a chance, the burger would be a single bite for this enthusiastic eater.

When Miley was fully awake and aware, it was time to go shopping. A new life, a new name, and now a new collar. Quality Supply was our favorite farm and ranch supply store because they would let your dog accompany you into the store to shop so long as your canine friend was well-behaved and leashed.

Miley bounded joyously into the store. Fearless about walking up to a stranger and nudging their hand for a pet, she was delighted by this place with so many hands. Working in Quality Supply was my friend Dawn, another Doberman owner and lover. Someone who really understands what a Dobie is all about. "Oh, look at her! Hi, baby! Can you have a cookie?" And so Miley's first shopping experience went, with Dawn cooing at her and spoiling her with dog biscuits to welcome her. Miley was now making plenty of good human friends. Her manners were impeccable in the store and as a result, she was winning the hearts of all who met her.

We walked back to the dog collar section where I took two down from the rack, a three-quarter-inch wide brown leather collar with a brass buckle and a one-inch wide black collar with a shiny silver buckle.

"Miley, you are pretty good at choosing things. How would you like to pick your new collar?" Though she was listening to every word I said, she was distracted by all the people that could and *should* be petting her. For her this place was one big meet and greet. So this time it would be my choice.

The black collar was a nice contrast to her milk chocolate colored fur, but the leather was stiff and it seemed a bit too large and masculine for her small body. The brown one was more pliant and it had a pretty brass buckle that appeared more feminine. It would look great with a brass name plate. Miley gave it a quick nod of agreement.

With that decision made, we wandered the rows of dog supplies allowing her the time she needed to sniff every bag of kibble and box of biscuits in the aisle. I let Miley choose some treats for the other dogs, since they would know by smell everywhere she had been, and we didn't want any jealousy. She chose braided rawhides. Pretty and tasty to dogs!

After we checked out and Miley got her Quality Supply cookie for good behavior, we went straight to the engraver's. I took the new collar in so I could match the brass plate to it. Once it was chosen, I wrote out what I wanted it to say:

"MILEY"

J. Fullerton

[Phone number]

It would be engraved and attached to the collar and ready to be picked up later that day. Simply stated, it linked us *togetherforever*.

Since our dogs are never collared at home, they only wear their collars when we leave our property. That meant some aspects of the new collar were symbolic, representative of a new start, of a commitment, like a wedding ring. "I take you, Miley, to be my dog for better or for worse." Gone were the names she couldn't relate to, the collar that caused so much pain, the poor diet, the cramped quarters, the cold, the heat, and the unhappiness. The motto for the rest of her life was to be

"Live for the joy of the day!" Perhaps she could teach us this more enlightened attitude. An attitude dogs are masters of.

Jeanie Notti- Fullerton

Chapter 12

Mustang Mania

On Friday of the next week, Miley was scheduled to see Dr. Patti Prato, our veterinary chiropractor, who was forty five miles away in Missoula. Since Toots went to work with her Dad on Fridays, I decided to take all three reds to Missoula with me that day. I loaded them into my Mustang. Hatchbacks are great. The only trouble was Angus took up all the space in the hatch himself. That didn't leave a lot of alternative space, so the girls sat together in the front seat, which Sophie was NOT used to sharing. She had always ridden the 'shotgun' position, and she wasn't going to be demoted from there. It was a position which had given her the freedom to curl up in the seat if she felt like it. Now she wasn't alone in her seat. And Miley seemed fine with the situation.

Things started out all right until we discovered Miley had an obsession with pine trees. Every time we would get near a stand of pine trees along the way, she would start howling and panting and bouncing around. This would get Sophie all stirred up, and she would join her. It became ridiculous. It was like being caught in a rock polishing tumbler. I would have to pull over because it wasn't safe for me to drive with dogs hopping from the front to the back and from the back to the front repeatedly. I was exhausted by the time we finally made it to Missoula. Meanwhile, big easy-going Angus just laid there, sweet, quiet, and well-behaved while being trodden on in the mayhem of these hyperkinetic girls.

It was a relief to get to the clinic, unload Miley, and go downstairs into the calm and quiet of the chiropractic office. It took a few minutes for Miley to settle down to this new experience of a chiropractic office with couches a dog could sit on and carpeting instead of slick floors. "Aunt" Patti didn't handle her like the veterinarians she was used to. She touched Miles all over from front to back with her kind and gentle hands, and what she discovered, besides a spine like disconnected jigsaw puzzle pieces needing to be aligned, was a dislocated hip. As she said, not clinically dislocated. Not the kind that is out of the socket. But the hip was not straight in the socket. We speculated on how this may have happened; could she have been hit by a car? Kicked by a large animal? Anything was possible. With one quick move Patti popped that hip straight and like a miracle, the limp disappeared. It was amazing. I was SO grateful. And Miley's new "Aunt" Patti did this as a blessing to her for surviving the hard times with a good attitude and landing in a soft place.

As a treat for them after waiting in the car so long, I decided to take all the canine kids to PetSmart. On the way, we drove past Home Depot--and there I had a profound moment of déjà vu...

It was a little over a year before that I had taken my new puppy Sophie in to Missoula to meet a friend of mine and to get the puppy out to socialize. On that day we came around the corner by Home Depot and there was a woman walking two Dobermans. A large black male and a small red female... On seeing them we pulled over, I rolled down the passenger window, and called out to her, "Do you mind if I ask where you got your dogs?"

At that moment her dogs erupted into snarling, growling, barking, out-of-control beasts. They dragged the woman to my car and they hit the side of the Mustang so hard I was sure they had dented it. All the while saliva was flying and all their teeth were showing. It was very frightening. I quickly called out, "Sorry!" and drove away until it was safe to stop and roll up my window. Puppy Sophie was traumatized by it. Her eyes were huge, she was pressed up against me, and she was shaking all over. I told her that was a bad owner, and those were troubled dogs, and assured her that she would not end up like that.

In my déjà vu moment I realized that was "Lucky" I had seen. Then I distinctly remembered seeing the big motor home and the unkempt woman. Oh, little girl...our paths have crossed before. I wish I could have stepped in then to save you another year of grief.

We made our trips into PetSmart to socialize. One at a time with the Mom. I didn't know how Miley would do in a situation where she was meeting other dogs in public. As it turned out, she liked this very much, but not because of meeting dogs. She liked that all the employees there carried cookies in their pockets and made a big deal out of her, admiring her collar, telling her she was beautiful. Happy people and happy, well-mannered dogs are always beautiful. You would have thought Miley was running for public office the way she could shake hands and kiss babies endlessly. And I was just her humble campaign manager who booked her appearances. She was being a great Doberman ambassador!

Sophie, on the other hand, strutted her stuff in the store to all the oohs and ahs you would expect for a title winner in a beauty pageant. She was blessed with limitless self-esteem. She didn't wait for people to offer her a cookie, she knew where all the cookie dishes were in the store, and she pulled me to them, jumped on the counter and helped herself to one. Apparently she believed beauty queens were entitled. And as her makeup artist and wardrobe manager I simply stood back and smiled while she soaked up the praise of her admirers. As we walked out of the store a little boy pointed to her and said to his mother, "Look, Mommy! That lady has a deer!" The similarity was indeed remarkable. And she was certainly a dear.

Angus just made people gasp, as a hundred pound beefcake like him would. He walked in a room and people scattered because he was so imposing. And intimidating. It was like walking into a club with my very own bouncer. Most people gathered their children, clutched them to their sides, and avoided coming down the same aisle we were in. However, one courageous lady came running up to us and asked if her children could pet my Scooby Doo dog. I couldn't break her heart by telling her that Scooby is a Great Dane, so I said yes. Angus tolerated it very well with an occasional eye roll in my direction. He had too much humility to understand the adoration being heaped on him.

You would have thought all this excitement may have taken the edge off their energy and might make the ride home quieter. But no. If anything it was worse. I was constantly pushing one dog or another into the back, pulling over to stop their barking and whining, chastising them for their restlessness.

By the time we got home I felt as if I'd been dragged behind a wagon train from St. Louis to Sutter's Mill during the gold rush. I was doubting my sanity. I didn't question my judgment for having these three Dobermans. I loved them, each and every one for just who they were. Collectively, however, something had to change. I needed to be able to take them places without it becoming a fiasco.

I told Marty how my day had gone, though I'm sure he could tell just by looking at me. He was sympathetic, but, being a guy, to him the solution was a bigger car. He couldn't run for the newspaper ads fast enough to begin shopping for a Ford Explorer--which he had been wanting and now had an excuse for! I loved my sports car. It was really my kind of car. It defined me. I didn't want to drive a great big SUV. But I didn't want a repeat of the chaos of today, either. We'll see...

Jeanie Notti- Fullerton

Chapter 13

A Family Complete

Marty and I had always wanted a big family. Four seemed the correct number of children. We carefully planned to have a child five years after we were married and that's what we did. Economics, social consciousness, and personal circumstances kept us from having more than one. But that one, Benjamin, or Benj as we called him, was the light of our lives. Naturally children grow up, move out, get married, and have children of their own. Often that leaves their parents feeling alone and without definition or purpose. That is where Marty and I eventually found ourselves.

When Benj was sixteen years old we got Toots for him. She was the product of a sweet black and rust Doberman who had been abandoned with seven puppies, locked in a house to starve when her owners moved away. When the neighbor girls heard the mother dog barking wildly in the empty house the sheriff's office was called, and she and her beautiful mixed-breed puppies were all rescued. They were taken to the animal shelter and were then fostered in a private home until they were old enough for adoption. We got Toots through the local Humane Association when she was seven weeks old. With her dark brown eyes and glossy black fur, it was obvious that her dad was a black Labrador. She was perfect in every way. Dobradorable. She became Benj's "chick magnet" that he took everywhere with him.

The Providential Doberman

Early on she learned to love doing "guy stuff." She wasn't cut out to be a hunting dog, but she was the best companion you could ever have and was willing for any sort of activity. We all became equally attached.

When Toots came into our family, she joined my gorgeous German Shepherd/Husky cross named Lady Anne. Very feminine, sweet, and tender, Lady was a shy, non-demanding dog. As a puppy she had tremendous fears. When I ran into my veterinarian friend, Dr. Brophy, while out with Lady for a mountain hike, he said to just take her everywhere with us to socialize her. So that's exactly what we did. Whether we were going to town or on a trip, Lady Anne was our constant sidekick. Her favorite place was Glacier Park where she spent a considerable amount of time trying to get me to come out of Lake McDonald by swimming out and circling me until I grabbed her tail and let her tow me back to shore.

For several years Lady Anne was our only dog and she was a delight. She had a keen sense of logic we could never argue with. I tried to teach her to fetch. She did very well on the first throw, but if I threw the Frisbee a second time Lady decided I must want it out there and she would refuse to fetch it back. Nope, only one fetch per game, if we couldn't hold onto our stuff it was not her problem!

She taught us well.

Lady garnered attention everywhere we went because she was so incredibly beautiful and soft natured. Several times we were stopped and asked if we would be interested in parting with her by people who would have taken her home with them in a heartbeat. Never would that happen. I loved her so. Lady Anne was elegant and gracious as she welcomed little Toots.

Just ten months after we got Toots, Lady Anne died under tragic circumstances. I was devastated. While my heart was still longing for my beautiful dog, Benj decided not to compound my grief by taking Toots with him when he moved out a few months later. It was a good decision, since he moved to town, and she had only lived in the country. But Toots was a guy dog. She loved me dearly, but if she had to choose between being in the kitchen with me or in the garage with the dad, she invariably chose the garage and dad. Even if she came in with her glossy black satin fur covered with sawdust or motor oil, she still preferred the garage. I was terribly lonely for a dog companion of my own again.

That's when Cosette came to me. Her life with me was rich and full, and she was a pampered, maybe even spoiled girl. Once again, I had someone to go nearly everywhere with me. And when we weren't together, when I was at work, I eagerly looked forward to going home. Those were defining moments. One night I worked an event that kept me out until 12:30 am. As I came up the driveway there she was, sitting in the moonlight in my parking spot, awaiting my arrival. She wasn't going to bed without me.

Cosette was the love of my life, my soul mate, filling the void of both, my lost Lady Anne and my lost motherhood. We were entirely devoted to one another almost to the exclusion of everyone else. She made me laugh and made me cry. I don't know if she realized that I was in a constant fight for her life. She took over my heart, my soul, my couch, and the foot of my bed.

Cosette died on September 8, 2001, just three days before the tragedy of the Twin Towers in New York City. When she died I didn't think I would survive it. The grief and loss were so all consuming. I couldn't eat or sleep. All I could do was curl up in a fetal position and cry endlessly. And then the whole world went into mourning...

Again I was alone. Toots also felt the power of loss, and she was lonely for someone of her own kind to lie on the porch and discuss life with. When Sophie came in November, we rejoiced for the new energy. She was full of good health and joy and puppy breath. So two months later when her breeder, Joanne, called and offered to gift us with her brother we said yes. This was a new experience for us; we had never had three dogs before. It took some adjusting to, since we had to be conscious to divide our attentions evenly. Nor had we ever had a male dog join our family. In fact Marty had held an adamant stand against male dogs all our married life...until he fell in love with Sophie. And this boy had been Sophie's best friend, her sidekick. Who wouldn't want another pup like her around?

Angus brought a whole new dimension to our lives. A great big, easy-going love sponge, he lived to be near any one of us. When Joanne offered him to us it was because all the people who had been interested in him wanted him either for a show dog or for protection. She had fallen in love with him early on and knew he wasn't geared for either. As she put it, "All he wants is to be loved and to lay his life down for someone he loves." She really knew her puppies.

However, Angus did not make such a great impression on his new doctor. At five and a half months old he hadn't really been socialized yet so he was unused to strangers handling him. As Dr. Hans went over him he reacted badly to having his hind end touched and nearly nipped the vet. I was shocked and I scolded him. Hans told me months later that he was worried about me taking on this powerful dog. He knew that I was a soft, gentle dog owner, not the Alpha bitch of my own dog pack, and I'm sure he was concerned about how I was going to get a handle on this boy's behavior.

As with Lady Anne, the trick was to take him out. I would take him for walks down Main Street with a handful of dog cookies in my pocket, and I would ask strangers if they would mind giving one to my dog. I would ask him to sit pretty, sniff their hand, and then he would get a cookie. He became quite the social butterfly because of it, assuming everyone had a treat for him. We also stopped at the vet clinic regularly just to get weighed and get a treat from Hans' assistants. By the time he was a year and a half old and Hans told me of his former concern, he was quick to say what a nice job we'd done in socializing him.

Angus had to be the smiliest Doberman we'd seen yet. And at one hundred plus pounds he'd better be good natured, friendly, and loveable! By the time Caleb-whose-name-means-dog was walking, the little guy was very taken with Angus. One day he toddled over to Angus, grabbed his nose, and proceeded to twist it off his face! Before I could extract the toddler's hand from the dog's snout his head was turned quite sideways trying to keep up with the torsion of his nose. But he never let out a peep or made any act of self-protection whatsoever. His eyes just opened wider and wider! After that he did learn to keep his nose elevated beyond the reach of tiny Caleb, though. As Caleb got older, he decided Angus would be fun to ride, and he tried to straddle him every chance he got. And each time Angus would jump up and buck him off! For a while we thought Caleb was going to have a career on the rodeo circuit--bronc riding. Angus started looking at it as part of a game, too, and would set him up for the fall, since Caleb giggled hilariously after each unsuccessful "ride."

By the time Miley came to live with us, we had become pretty settled as a family of five. My Mom said we were like people who planned to have two children but then had a couple of unplanned children, too. Nevertheless, I was more than willing to round our family up to six. It did make life somewhat more complicated, for sure. But wasn't this the big family we had always wanted?

Having only one child ourselves, I never understood how anyone with multiple children could love them all equally. Wasn't that first one just the most amazing, incredible human ever born? How could you ever top that feeling, that whole-hearted love? We had much to learn.

As it turns out, love is not divided, it is multiplied. You take no love away from one to give to the other. In fact, as we watched them together, as we all interacted as a family, our love reached new depths, new heights, new dimensions we couldn't have imagined. As we worked out the problems we really felt the responsibility of being parents. We protected them all equally. We did what was best for each as an individual, while also considering what was best for the group. We loved and respected each one for whom they were, as unique, not expecting them to be alike in any way except in their willingness to cooperate as a real family.

Marty and I loved having this big family. We were now complete. It was the most fulfilling feeling to come home to all these happy faces. To see them play together, to work out their positions and problems amongst themselves. To watch the interactions daily was such a joy. We had become parents to children who were to be with us their entire lives.

So the month after Miley joined us we bought a Ford Explorer, a car for a family of six, and a wire mesh divider to keep us all safe. I loved my Mustang and had at one time told Marty that if he wanted me to stay home and never go anywhere all he had to do was make me drive a station wagon. Because of my attachment to the sports car I had to reconcile this SUV to myself. So I took the Explorer to Sign Pro and had gold vinyl scroll work put on it to pretty it up, had the dog's names put on the back doors above the handles, and had "Ford Protection System by Doberman" written across the back side windows. We were now parents of four with the "station wagon" I thought I never wanted. And we were very happy.

Chapter 14

The "R" Word

A few weeks later, my friend Suzie invited me to lunch with her and her veterinarian friend, Dr. Linda Perry, at a local café. While we ate, we told animal stories back and forth until eventually we got to Miley's. I told of how we got her and what condition she was in. Then I told about her choosing her new name.

"Wait a minute!" the vet said. "A red Doberman named Lucky?"

"Yes."

"Was she living in a motor home with a big black male Doberman?"

"Yes."

"I know that dog!" she said.

"You do? Tell me how."

"The woman who owned her called me and we agreed to meet at the Laundromat on Main Street so I could give the dogs their annual vaccines. She got them out of the motor home, and they got away from her and ran all over Hamilton terrorizing the town. They wouldn't listen to her at all. In fact I thought the red female might be retarded. She didn't seem to know her own name or any commands. After an hour and a half of chasing them I finally left. I never did see her catch them."

I was aghast;this beautiful, intelligent dog child of mine, capable of choosing her own name, of charming the most hardened heart, retarded? What kind of state of mind must she have been in? What stress must she have been under to make her run from her circumstances so that she appeared to be mentally disabled? Certainly the woman inspired no loyalty from Dobermans. But there must have been some sort of psychological stress crack for her to act that way.

I wasn't offended. Dr. Perry certainly didn't say it to be insulting or hurtful. Quite the contrary, she just was expressing an impression she had gotten from the dog's behavior. I said, "I understand why you would think that. It's interesting how animals react to stress and pain, isn't it? Like with us, stress can change their personalities, numb their sensibilities, and make them act in ways that are totally out of character. This is one of the smartest dogs I've ever known. Miley was oppressed and abused and at any opportunity for freedom she made a run for it. When she finally got the love she needed and deserved she blossomed. Our love gave her the freedom to choose to return love,and to choose loyalty and obedience. I'm anxious to see who she'll be when she is totally healed from her wounds, both physical and emotional."

I took something valuable away from this conversation. The old adage "Never judge a book by its cover" became much clearer to me. The surface reactions of someone may not be what lies at their core. We are all affected by our environment, by the positive and negative energies we are surrounded by on a day to day basis. And it shows. But clear away the negativity and you may be surprised to find the beauty that lies beneath the surface. To judge by the appearance or immediate behavior limits your possibilities of seeing that beauty.

I was blessed. On a cold winter day in December I had seen Miley's true beauty. It may have been in a ragged package, but that was *not* the first thing I saw.

While meditating on this I realized I had learned this lesson before - the day I chose to bring Sophie home from Washington. Even as a tiny puppy, Sophie was able to see through my ragged, grief-worn exterior and into my heart to the person I am. The person who needed help to survive. She saw the interior beauty of a gentle but broken heart. I'll never forget that incredible experience. And now I was paying it forward to Miley.

Chapter 15

Books and Their Covers

The first weekend of November, 2001, we traveled six hundred miles to Silverdale, Washington to pick up a beautiful black and rust Doberman puppy. I'd lost Cosette just two months before and ten days later I began emailing and talking on the phone with this puppy's breeders, Joanne and Ralph Duncan. They had sent me the most adorable photos of my puppy, a little black bundle of joy. But often in the photos was this other face. A little red puppy girl with a hot pink ribbon and laser beam eyes that were always staring at the camera. Homely by comparison to the little black, I often said, "Well, I know which puppy I'm *not* coming home with!"

Ralph and Joanne graciously insisted we spend the night with them after the twelve hour trip. They wanted us to get really well acquainted with the puppies so we were sure to make the correct decision. When we arrived at their home, the puppies were in a pen in the kitchen. The first to come to the front of the pen was the red female with the pink ribbon and laser beam eyes from the photos. But as soon as she got to the front the other puppies crowded in under her and pushed her to the back, and she ended up sitting quietly against the wall staring at us with those compelling eyes.

That evening we sat in the middle of the kitchen floor surrounded by bouncy, happy, healthy Doberpuppies. While the other puppies were playing tough and tumble games, the little red female with the pink ribbon came over to me, sat down beside me, and whacked me with her paw. I glanced down at her little eleven week old face and smiled and told her to scoot along and play. She just looked me straight in the eye and whacked me again. Since my chosen puppy was busy playing I went ahead and picked this girl up. At that instant it was as though peace descended on me from heaven. There was no explanation for it. Her energy just took my pain away. She bored a hole through me with her laser beam eyes and looked straight into my soul. I could tell she had everything it would take to help heal me, including a willingness to try.

But I was resistant. She wasn't what I wanted to see visually. I have never thought the red dogs were as showy, not what you think of when you think Doberman. Suddenly I realized what I was doing...she wasn't my beloved Cosette. Or my darling Messina, my precious first Dobie. Was that fair to do to another dog? Put these kinds of expectations on the next puppy? Maybe it was time to rethink my motives and desires...

Then something happened that we'd never seen before. A squabble broke out between two little puppies in the corner. The pink ribboned puppy I was holding struggled to get out of my arms, rushed to the corner, and threw her body in between the squabbling pair to break up their argument. As soon as all was calm she came back to me and whacked me again with her little paw. A peacemaker.A healer. I picked her up and kissed her little forehead.

Joanne told me this laser-eyed girl was the firstborn and the leader of the puppy pack. Brave, she was always out in front on their outdoor adventures with her second-born brother close behind. At the same time she was sensitive and easily pushed to the back of the crowd where she sat on the fringe and observed. I could relate.

I didn't sleep at all that night. I tossed and turned and cried and paced. Joanne had already made out the papers for the little black. I got up in the middle of the night and went out to the pen where the puppies were sleeping and just stared at them. How could I choose? Marty woke up when I came back to bed, and I presented him with the same question. He wisely said, "Sometimes you have to see with your heart and not with your eyes."

He was absolutely right. This red puppy with the laser beam eyes didn't judge me by my sad, tired, and worn appearance. How dare I judge her for not being the color I had envisioned my new puppy? She was a person just as I am, deserving of respect for whom she was, not just how she looked. She had willingly offered up her heart in service to me. And I had to admit that our hearts had collided in something more powerful than nuclear fusion.

The next morning I told Joanne I had changed my mind. I wanted the little red girl with the pink ribbon. Every time I held her I got the same descending peace, and it was a comfort beyond belief. I had chosen the black puppy's name, Seraphina, but it didn't suit this girl. I asked her to change the name to Sophie. And her AKC registry name from the Voyager litter was to be Voyager to My Heart. Lesson learned...

Jeanie Notti- Fullerton

Chapter 16

Like She Needed Another Hole in Her Head

Our winters can be long in Montana, and it isn't unusual to have some pretty heavy snow storms as late as March, April, or even May. And we have been known to have an occasional bout of winter in June - June-uary. In 2003 our heaviest snow storm of the winter came the first week in March. By the time we were ready for dinner on that Friday evening there were over sixteen inches of new snow on the ground. The county road department was out plowing and sanding the roads, and we were battening our hatches and resting up for a long weekend of shoveling. All four dogs had chosen to go out with Marty to feed our Tennessee Walking horses, Sunny (Chariot Sun Lady), Starr (Starrlet O'Hara), and Queen (Delta Queen), and do the chores, even though with their short Doberman hair they were usually averse to cold and snow. While they were out, I fixed their dinner and was ready to feed them when they returned.

When Marty came in he didn't notice that only three of the canine kids were with him. As I was getting ready to set their dishes down, I saw that Miley had not come in. I ran to the back door to call for her, but she was waiting for me to open the door. The dog yard gate was shut, and she couldn't come in the dog door, so she had a light layer of snow on her back from waiting for a minute or two for the door to open to her. She didn't seem cold, but she was relieved that she wasn't forgotten. She shook the powdered sugar dusting of snow flakes off as I set her dish down. She ate in peace while we sat down to our own dinner.

After dinner we were all gathered close to the wood stove watching television when I glanced down at Miss Miley. Something was wrong. The inner eyelid of her right eye was showing. I turned a brighter light on and I screamed.

"OH MY GOD!! Miley's skull is broken!" I thought I was going to pass out. Above her right eye was a deep dent in her head. I knew immediately what had happened. The horses get squirrelly when it snows, often bucking and kicking and romping around to get the snow off their backs. She had gotten in the way of a flying hoof and the deep snow prevented her from avoiding the impact. She'd only been with us for two months and she wasn't as horse smart as the others.

I ran to the telephone and called the emergency number to find out who the vet on call was. It was Dr. Joe Melnarik, an experienced veterinarian and an easy-going Montanan. I called him, frantic and crying, and he said to meet him at the clinic as soon as we could get there. We threw our coats on, and Marty picked Miley up and ran her to the truck. Marty put it in four wheel drive, and away we went as fast as thirty five miles an hour could get us the twelve miles there. I held her in my arms and sobbed the entire way in, blubbering about how I'd promised her no more pain and now look! How could I have let this happen? Surely she would be brain damaged! What if we had to have her euthanized because of it? I'd never forgive myself. I called my mom on the way, and she said she'd meet us at the clinic, too. I was admittedly hysterical by the time we got there.

When we arrived, Dr. Joe was shoveling the snow from the clinic walks. As we got out of the truck and set Miley down, he was watching her.

"Yep. She got kicked in the head."

The calmness in his voice was amazing to me, and it pulled the plug on my hysteria. He took us in the back door of the clinic without any hint of this being a critical, emergency situation. He picked her up and put her on the table, and I held her there while he examined her thoroughly. As he did he told us that he had seen this several times before in cattle dogs, mostly heelers, who got a little too close to the hooves and got kicked.

Then he said, "She's going to be fine. Dog's heads are built differently than ours. This area is actually her sinus cavity."

I don't know that I have ever been more relieved in my life. I laid my head on the table and wept, this time the tears of relief. When I looked up my mom was crying, too. Mom had never owned a dog of her own, but she had certainly felt the love from mine, and it grieved her to think that little Miley could have yet another injury.

"She'll probably have a pretty good headache for a few days, and if you want you can have surgery done on her to wire the pieces together. But even without surgery she'll heal up and be fine." With that he went and got some medication for her pain to complement the homeopathic remedies she would be getting from me, and away we went.

We kept Miles quiet for days. We made a brief stop on Monday to show Dr. Hans what happened, and he advised we not have surgery done on the fracture. The pieces of bone were too small to wire, and if left alone the injury would heal with only a small bump.

The other dogs knew Miley was hurt, and they didn't press her to play. When I had to go to work for a few

119

hours the next week, I left her with mom where she was pampered, as all grand-dogs should be. It was a long time before she ventured near horses again, and we were grateful for that.

Three months after Miley came to live with us, she still had one stubborn puncture wound on the left side of her chest that refused to heal no matter what I doctored it with. One evening while I was sitting on the floor petting her I noticed a drop of pus in the middle of the wound. I grabbed a tissue and covered the wound and gave it a good squeeze, thinking I would just get more pus. Instead, to my horror, I felt something hard. Out of the hole came a piece of wood, as big around as a pencil and an inch and a quarter long! It had been imbedded deep in her flesh for many, many months! Right above her heart. Her body was finally strong enough to expel it.

Now she was exorcised of all the pain of the past, her healing would soon be complete. And with the flesh set free of the obstacles to healing, her psyche healed too. Bless her little broken head...

Chapter 17

Racing with Speed Goats

Miley settled into our routine very well. We could trust her outside without a leash except for one thing; she wanted to go mousing in the neighbor's field. Normally that would appear to be a good thing, a dog that wanted to help hold down the rodent population. Except that our neighbor doesn't like dogs, particularly not Dobermans, and he most especially didn't want her digging out mouse holes in his horse pasture. We couldn't blame him for that. So we put up nearly a quarter mile of electric fence to keep our dogs out of there. Problem solved.

Unquestionably, though, these dogs needed some sort of vigorous exercise to keep them healthy and happy. The girls especially needed the opportunity to run and stretch their legs to the full. They were true athletes and we had to figure out a way to take them on the back roads and allow them to run some of that excess energy off safely.

We enjoyed taking the dogs to the mountains to exercise. We had learned early on that being in the woods was therapeutic for Miley. It was a nice thing for outdoorsy Sophie, who we often called the Florence Griffith Joyner of Dobermans. She was as elegant as a whitetail deer when she ran. Miley, on the other hand, was more eager than elegant, and far more vocal. From the instant she saw a pine tree a glazed look came over her face, and she would go into an altered state of mind, unable to contain herself. She started whining, crying, barking, and howling to be let out of the truck to run. Over the next few weeks we tried every imaginable alternative calming agent on her and no herbal supplement or homeopathic remedy or essential oil worked. Even with sedation she simply did the same behaviors slower. So we gave up trying to suppress her abundant enthusiasm, and instead we saw that she got the exercise it would take to calm her. As soon as they were let out of the truck, Miley would bark and run up the road as fast as her little compromised feet and legs could carry her. Running on the backroads was ecstasy for her.

One of our favorite drives was to the Big Hole Valley, a beautiful high valley surrounded by majestic mountains where you could drive back in to the lakes to camp. We decided we would take a drive one late spring weekend to a lake I had never been to, Musigbroad Lake, and see what the camp sites were like. There had been a forest fire up there the year before, and they had made some improvements to the campground while the firefighters were encamped in the vicinity for several weeks.

So we packed a picnic lunch and loaded the dogs into the pickup topper and away we went. By this time we knew what to expect from our noisy Miley girl. When we got to the top of Chief Joseph Pass, the half-way point on our journey, we would let them out, and we'd walk down the cross-country ski trail while they ran around and got some of that initial energy worn off so they could calm down for the second leg of the journey.

When we got to the Forest Service section of the lake road we let them out on the road for their marathon. They would stay in front of the truck, and we would just drive the speed they ran. Their joy of running was incredible. Because the traffic on the roads we took them on was very low and very slow, they were safe to just lope along in the fresh air, occasionally deviating off the road to chase a chipmunk into a hole or a squirrel up a pine tree. It was the thing that made the Dober-girls the happiest. We didn't have to worry about them running into wildlife because the wildlife could hear Miley barking with joy a mile away and would be long gone by the time she got there. Obnoxious? Yes.

We leashed the dogs when we got to the campground, and they took us for a nice drag, er, walk, on the lake trail. It was a beautiful area and several people were camped there. After our so-called walk we found a nice place down by the creek to have our lunch. The high mountain air was good for the lungs, and the scenery was good for the soul. The spring sun was dazzling and warm, and the dogs found some soft new grass to nap in after they had a bite to eat with us. You could hear birds singing to their mates as they flitted here and there for nesting materials. Big fat bumble bees were lunching deep in the bells of the wildflower blossoms. The air was sweet with freshness. We took the opportunity to bask in the golden rays of sunlight and admire the pale green new growth on the fir trees as white popcorn clouds floated lazily across the robin's egg blue sky. We were in close proximity to heaven.

Life was so good. Miley had healed well from all the injuries, including the fractured skull. Her hair was coming in on her head and her chest. The scars were fading. And she was as happy as a dog can get. She had freedom to choose to be loyal. She no longer needed to be leashed to stay by our sides. She wanted to be with us and made sure we were never out of her field of vision. And we were feeling great about what we had been able to do for her. Sophie loved her. They would play several times a day and then find a sunbeam to nap together in. Angus had adjusted to being growled at one minute and then being licked and asked to play the next. Bless his heart for being such an easy-going guy.

Jeanie Notti- Fullerton

On our way back out of the woods we decided to let the girls run just a little farther. As we got to a bend in the road where we were going to load them up again, Miley's head shot up. She had caught a whiff of something. Suddenly we saw what it was. A pronghorn antelope. By the time we slammed on the brakes and jumped out to call her back it was too late. She was off like a shot and Sophie right behind her. We weren't concerned about the speed goat (a nickname for antelope); he was toying with them. If she thought she could ever catch up to him she hadn't been watching PBS. The beautiful pronghorn antelope can sprint as fast as sixty miles per hour or run a sustained thirty miles an hour for miles and have been known to race with cars along the highway. But we were worried because they crossed off of Forest Service ground onto private land and any rancher has a right to shoot a dog if it is chasing livestock on his property. We were panicked.

We drove down the road calling and honking and trying to get them back. We would stop and whistle and yell. But they were focused on the big race. We were sick. We felt like the most irresponsible dog owners in the world to have let this happen. They were never out of sight, but they were a long way off. We turned around and went a couple of miles back up the road, then

126

turned once again and headed back down. It was an interminable few minutes.

Suddenly Sophie popped up on the road, panting heavily. We praised her for coming back to us but as we loaded her in the truck we chastised her seriously for not listening to us. Her obedience was something we had been able to count on in the rehabilitation of Miley. They were devoted to one another and we looked to Sophie to set the example. But now what? In putting her into the truck we had lost sight of Miley.

We continued the drive back down the road, and, as we rounded the bend, there she was sitting just as pretty as a picture in the middle of the road at the exact spot she was when she first spotted the antelope. Once again we had a rush of relief. I cried as we jumped out of the truck to load her. When we put her into the topper we scolded her to let her know what she had done was very bad, how unhappy and disappointed we were with her, and she took our words straight to her heart. We could tell it hurt her to hurt us. And I could see that my tears had a deep effect on her. It was a lesson she would never forget.

Miley was street smart. She had raced miles with an antelope across the sage brush, and all the while she knew exactly where we were and how to reconnect with us. We would also keep the lesson of this forever.

They had done something very bad, illegal, and we were responsible for their actions. We had to rethink how we would allow them to run so as to not endanger any wildlife, anyone's livestock, or them. Just because it turned out fine (we could see the antelope off grazing, completely undisturbed by the incident) didn't mean it was fine. We would figure it out. Running was too important to these dogs' joy of living to not find a way to allow them that opportunity. And their happiness meant our happiness.

Chapter 18

Search and Rescue

With patience we let our track and field athlete dogs
know we would take them for runs only if they would
stay with us. They loved a mid-winter trip to Como
Lake where they could run unimpeded amongst the big
exposed shoreline rocks and explore along the edge of
the lake. Meanwhile, we would build a roaring campfire
and roast some hot dogs for all of us. The running kept
them warm and they liked the feel of the smooth snow
as opposed to gravel on their feet.

On an exquisite winter day when the snow was
glistening like strewn diamonds across white velvet we
took one such trip to the lake. After a little picnic, we
decided to let them run as we drove from the boat
launch on one side of the lake to the beach on the other,
a short semi-loop. At one point the road forks, one
direction going to the beach, and the other going off into
the mountains. When we got to that point the girls took
the wrong road. We stopped and called them but only
Miley came back around to join us. We called and called
and no Sophie. Then suddenly there was no Miley
either. Great. Where had they gone?

We drove back the hundred feet or so to where the road
branched and went a little ways up in the other
direction. The snow was so deep we couldn't drive very
far. We called and called...and called some more. No

dogs. My mouth went dry with fear and the tears welled up. I didn't dare speak out loud the words I was thinking: leg snare traps. The stories of dogs caught in them are horrifying and gruesome...death-dealing. I hate the thought of any animal experiencing such cruelty. I didn't think they were allowed so close to a recreation area, but I wasn't sure. I could feel myself go back and forth between holding my breath and hyperventilating.

As we came back down we saw some people coming from the other side of the lake. We stopped them and asked them if they had seen a couple of red Dobermans...they had...at the boat launch. Sure enough, there they were;sitting, waiting for us to come pick them up. Miley had found Sophie and taken her back where they began. She knew we would figure it out. She had taught us well. Sophie was not street smart; she had no reason to be. Someone had always taken care of her. And now, along with mom and dad, she had a big sister to do that for her, too. An absolutely astonishing big sister.

We hugged and kissed them and praised them for working out a solution to being lost. What happened this time was far different from their not listening to us in the past. This time they zigged and we zagged and we simply got separated. But it was a frightening incident, and my imagination took me to places I hope never to actually visit.

Once again we were put to the test as to how we could allow them to get the exercise they needed while keeping them safe. Fortunately, these dogs were brilliant, and their desire for our approval was more important to them than even their need to run. So they learned to listen more carefully to us on our outings. Often we used our bicycles to accompany them. And they never again were out of our sight in the woods.

Miley was our hero, a champion in a crisis. A girl who loved her freedom, but loved all of us even more. We were so fortunate to have her love.

Chapter 19

The Woobie

We discovered Miley's need for a "woobie" early on when the foot end of the comforter on my bed was wadded up and soaking wet one day. It wasn't urine; it was saliva. I didn't say anything, I just observed. That evening, as I was reading in bed, I peered over the top of my book and watched her as she pulled the comfy up, tugging and positioning it with her mouth until it was shaped like a nipple, then she sucked and nursed on it with her eyes closed, making little puppy whimpers as her head bobbed methodically, just like any nursing puppy.

At first it just broke our hearts to watch her. We had never seen or even heard of this behavior in dogs. We had seen it with cats, but not dogs. Was she weaned too soon? Was she orphaned? Was she abandoned? We would never know the answers to any of these questions because the active search I had done on the tattoo in her ear had turned up nothing. I had breeders in the United States and Canada asking their peers all over if they knew anything about this set of numbers and letters and it remained a mystery. And so did Miley's increasingly distant past. Quite sometime later I found out that laboratories also use ear tattoos for identification. This was information I would never pursue.

What was obvious was that she found comfort from nursing, and chewing, on a comforter. She was not unlike a child who sucked her thumb while dragging her blanket around. We never ridiculed or laughed at or humiliated her in any way for this odd habit. It was her way of easing stress, of relaxing.

I staked claim to my own bed cover and found some older, faded, cotton comfies for her. I cut them into quarters, hemmed the edges, washed them in non-toxic soap, double rinsed them, and dried them on the clothesline so she wouldn't be ingesting harmful chemicals. She loved having her very own possessions.

Miley's woobies ended up having multi-purposes for her. They were not only good for sucking, chewing, and pulling the stuffing out of, but also for shaking back and forth wildly, for dragging all over the countryside, and for rousing games of tug o' war. And when the games were over it was good to nap on.

If I would try to put her woobie into the wash I had to sneak it while she was busy chewing a bone or some other absorbing task and put it directly into the washer. If it was dropped into a pile of dirty clothes it was rescued as soon as I turned my back. Then I would have to wait until she finished comforting her woobie to sneak it back into the wash.

We had a woobie with us on every trip we ever took. We wouldn't have risked the potential of separation anxiety from leaving it. Interestingly, Miley wasn't selfish with her woobie. It became something the other dogs not only accepted but also seemed to enjoy lying on occasionally. Even though it was important to her to have ownership, Miley didn't seem to mind sharing her abundance, perhaps thinking it was a universally comforting piece of fabric. Often we had multiple woobies lying around the house and rolled up in the toy basket, so it was easy to find one at any given moment. When she thought she needed a specific woobie that someone was occupying, she came and told me instead of taking matters in her own teeth, and I would extract the woobie from under whoever was on it.

Strangely, it was difficult for us to throw the woobies away when the time had come. Though her woobies were beloved, Miley disemboweled them fairly quickly. When they became nothing but a mass of holes held together by some random stitching or a knot with shreds of chewed fabric hanging off, it was time to salute its faithful service and sentimentally send it off to Woobieland.

We provided many entertaining toys for our dogs, and Miley seemed to enjoy them most of all. She would fetch, play with, and chew a tennis ball until she punctured it (in exactly seven minutes), and very much enjoyed silencing the squeaker in a squeaky toy. Playing catch was always good sport...one Sophie was envious of since she never could figure out exactly where her elegantly long nose actually began and ended so she could never catch very well. Popcorn would always bounce off her nose either before or after she had her mouth open.

The string tug, a sturdy version of a woobie tug, was everyone's favorite. Angus would get on one end of it and Miley on the other, and they would pull for all they were worth. Remarkably, he had met his match though she weighed thirty-five to forty pounds less than he did. Miley was as strong as steel cable and more determined than anyone else when it came to games.

But her woobie was special. Unique. A comforting scrap of comforter. We see it in children; they start out with a blanket (in my case a soft pink flannel "binky"). Then they graduate to some object, a little girl who carries her doll everywhere, a little boy who has a matchbox car in his pocket at all times. When do we outgrow this? Or do we just continue to transfer those same feelings to something else? For me, Miley became my woobie. A comforting friend who soothed my nerves and made me feel safe, warm, and relaxed. What more could anyone ask for?

Chapter 20

"I Would Lay My Life Down For You"

In June of 2003 we went to Billings, Montana, for an annual convention we were attending. We had for many years camped at the fairgrounds next to the Metra where the convention was held, as did several hundred other attendees. This was sure to be a challenging year for us, bringing four dogs along. We would have to keep them collared and leashed the entire four days, and it would be a lot of walking for us in order to get all of them enough exercise. But we certainly weren't going to leave them home with a sitter for that long.

When we arrived on Thursday in the early afternoon, there was a flurry of activity, with people positioning their campers and RV's and setting up tents. Friends we only got to see once a year milled around, greeting us with hugs, taking the time to catch up on how the past year had gone for each of us.

Once we got the camper all situated in our site, with the back of it edging a spacious lawn, I grabbed something to drink, a lawn chair, and Miley on her leash, and we went out to sit and enjoy the afternoon sun. We hadn't been out for more than a couple of minutes when an excited lady came striding in between our camper and the next with a sledge hammer in her hand and her hand held up shoulder height. She called out, asking if we knew the person she had borrowed the hammer from,

140

but as she approached Miley construed the gesture as aggression. She jumped up, put herself between me and the intruder, and, staring the lady straight in the eye, she let out a growl. The startled woman stopped in her tracks. She knew immediately that she had made a mistake by approaching too fast with what looked to a dog like a weapon.

I instantly put my hand on Miley, and it calmed her. I didn't scold her or discourage her behavior in any way. She was doing her job to perfection, protecting me from a perceived danger. The lady apologized profusely. I asked her to put the hammer down and meet my gallant dog who was willing to lay her life down for me. Miley was forgiving, as was in character for her to be, and, after sniffing the gal's hand, cordially offered to shake hands with her.

Miley was my champion. My protector. She made me feel safe when so little else did.

Over the long weekend in Billings, she and the other dogs made many new friends, including a couple of teenaged girls who loved nothing more than parading these powerful, impressive looking dogs around and showing them off. Two or three times a day they would come and take them walking or running all over the fairgrounds. It was good for everyone concerned. Miley loved teenaged girls as it turned out. Well, whom didn't she love?

The next year, 2004, on our way home from that same annual convention, we stopped for the night at a favorite campsite in the mountains near Wise River. In the morning we let the dogs out to have some freedom after being confined and leashed for four days. It was a gorgeous Montana morning, crisp, clear, with the melody of rushing water in the air. It was still spring and the scent of the new pine growth was strong. While I finished a leisurely breakfast, Marty decided to take a walk down to the creek with the canine kids.

A few minutes later there came a frantic scratching at the door of the camper. I opened it, and all three red Dober-kids came rushing in nearly knocking me over. They ran up on the bed and were staring out the window, serious faced, their almond-shaped eyes perfectly round with concern. When I looked out to see what was alarming them, I couldn't believe my eyes...there was Marty and Toots, being chased around a tree by an immense and very hostile mother moose!

Moose are nothing to fool around with. Big, powerful animals, they have killed many people, either by goring them or by overtaking them and stomping on them. And this mama was *mad*. No doubt she had hidden her baby down by the creek, and Marty and the dogs had come way too close, and now she was going to make them go away, if she had to kill them to protect her young.

As he gradually got closer to the camper, Marty began yelling and circling trees to keep the cow moose at bay. At just the right moment he and Toots made a run for it, and I opened the door so they could leap in. Undaunted by a little metal, the moose circled the camper several times, threatening and snorting to make sure we had all gotten the message to stay away from that section of the creek.

Toots had loyally stayed with Marty through the whole thing, ready to get stomped with him to help get him back to safety. She was willing to lay her life down for him.

Toots was Marty's champion. His protector.Helping him to be safe in an unsafe situation.

The reds had chosen not to enter a battle with one so formidable or to irritate the situation further by remaining outside. It was the course of wisdom to get out of the way. Or maybe they were just plain scared, and instead they retreated to mom, who was known for slaying dragons. Either way, everyone was safe and all had exercised good judgment. And that left the dad with a great moose story to tell his friends back home!

Chapter 21

What's an Issue or Twelve Between Friends?

Miley was a very complicated girl, full of issues that we had to meet face to face with every day. Some we only had to deal with occasionally. Like clipping toenails.

From the first day we saw her, when her nails were two inches long and deforming her feet, we knew there must be a problem. The bottom line was that she was terrified of the clippers and simply refused to allow her feet to be handled because of it. We had no way of knowing if this was related somehow to the broken toes, but there must have been horrible pain involved at some point for the reaction to the clippers to be so dramatic. Her pupils would dilate, and she would scream at the top of her lungs and throw herself around violently to get away from the toenail clippers. Nevertheless, it was crucial to her health to have her toenails clipped.

This situation was even more problematic than just Miley, because in order to keep the Dober-twins pretty "kitty paw" shaped feet it was essential to clip their toenails once a month. Miley was going to teach them all the wrong messages about nail grooming.

In the beginning I not only didn't want her to influence the other dogs, but I didn't want her to associate us with a procedure that was so traumatic for her. So I tried taking her to groomers. Each trip was its own Dante's

Inferno-like nightmare. I never had the nerve to take her back to the same groomer twice--not that we were invited to do so anyway. Besides, no one was ever able to really complete the job.

We tried doing it ourselves. It was a rodeo complete with bull-dogging, calf roping, steer wrestling, and bull riding, all with one singular small red Doberman. And there were no big, shiny, silver belt buckles at the end. Just a couple of broken down old cowboys who'd been bucked off and rolled in the dirt because they couldn't make it the whole eight seconds.

I would give her relaxing homeopathic remedies and run a bead of lavender oil down her back. We would do it after her bath, when the nails were soft from soaking in the water. We tried doing her nails after clipping the other dog's nails. We tried doing her first. We tried using a Dremel tool. We tried different kinds of clippers. We tried just hand filing. We tried bribing, distracting, coddling. Nothing improved our situation. It always ended up with Marty holding her on her back in his arms with her legs and feet straight up and a death grip around her chest while she flailed and I clipped as fast as I could. She broke his glasses once. Another time she threw herself so hard against the side of his head she broke his eardrum.

We were tired, injured, and frustrated.

Finally I took her into Dr. Hans' office. I explained the situation, and they were very sure they could get the job done. Seasoned professionals. They asked that I not be in the room, saying dogs act much better when their owners aren't hovering. So I sat just on the other side of the door and waited for the action to begin. And it did. I'm sure Miley could be heard for several blocks. From the room came noise that made me envision a Looney Toon cartoon featuring Dr. Hans Boer wrestling the Tasmanian devil, the air cluttered with the symbols of cursing -- *#@!! I thought I heard a clipper hit the wall.

After five minutes they all came out of the room, Miley virtually leaping into my arms with relief to see me. Dr. Hans and Natasha didn't look nearly as good as she did. Disheveled, sweaty, hair drooping, exhausted, they had gotten two toenails clipped. Hans advised a sedative if we were ever to get the job done, and suggested that I administer it a half hour before I bring her in again.

At this point we decided to risk life and limb and continue to do this job ourselves. I would give her the sedative and wait until it took effect...which it never fully did. I felt defeated by having to resort to something so drastic. There had to be a better way.

Miley had always been a dog whom could be reasoned with if you talked to her. So Marty and I took a different tactic, we talked her through it. If we only got one foot done at a time we accepted that as success. Our patience paid off. Over the course of time she came to understand that we were doing something good for her, and that she looked beautiful at the end of the process. So she eventually accepted our efforts graciously, without sedatives.

Miley also had some sort of neuropathy in her legs. There were times when she would lie on the bed at night and lick her delicate legs until they were soaking wet, whining all the while. At those times I would give her some homeopathic remedies, and put a dot of lavender oil at the base of her skull and on the top of her head. She would relax and be asleep in minutes. Then I discovered something effective that she just loved...ginger.

I'd gotten some ginger chews at the health food store and was eating one as I sat in bed reading one night. When I looked up she was staring at me with drool-cicles hanging at the corners of her mouth. I didn't think she would actually eat one, so I held it out for her to sniff. She quickly took it and chewed it up with relish. I gave her a second one and the next thing I knew she was sound asleep, relaxed, with no pain. After that I had to be careful not to leave a bag of them out where she could get them as she once ate a half pound of them, paper and all. They were bedtime treats and she loved them.

Stealing food was a particular talent Miley had perfected, probably during the hungry years. Anything and everything was fair game if it was left within Miley's reach. Dobermans are known for counter scanning and thievery anyway, then you add a little survival instinct on top of it and you had better be aware of what was within reach at all times. She was like the Artful Dodger, and they became our very own pack of Dickensonian pickpockets...

The fruit bowl was Angus' smorgasbord. He stole apples, bananas (which he learned to pull the stem off of and stand on to squeeze the fruit out of the peeling), pears, and even mangoes from it. Sophie liked sweets; molasses cookies, carrot cake, pumpkin pie, jelly beans and the like. Toots managed to steal a rib-eye steak, done medium-rare, from someone's plate on a camp trip. Miley went for the gold. She once got a beef sirloin roast out of the pan on the stove. Another time it was a perfectly golden browned, herb-encrusted, roasted chicken. She even swooped in and took a loaded burger right out of a friend's hand at a picnic. We were mortified. We understood the mindset, but that didn't make it less embarrassing or annoying. I could never get very angry with Miley for it. It was a survival mechanism. When I would scold her and put her in "time out", she looked horrified at upsetting me, but instinct would always override judgment in this area. We learned to be more mindful of what was available for stealing and keeping food out of reach.

Angus got the prize for gluttony, however, when he managed to get through an elaborately and carefully (we thought) constructed barricade in the back of my car and into the Costco loot. He ate eleven Costco blueberry muffins and two pounds of fig bars. One would think we would have to have his stomach pumped under those circumstances, but no. He didn't even act as if he had a bellyache, just a sugar high. Then the next day he threw up the equivalent of one blueberry muffin. So apparently his limit was two pounds of fig bars and only ten Costco blueberry muffins. Even Miley had to be impressed with that.

We used homeopathic remedies to deal with Miley's trauma issues. The remedy that helped her the most ended up being Belladonna, with some of its indications being reactiveness, dilated pupils and hot spots of inflammation. It calmed her sudden snappishness with Angus, making her less reactive, more patient and tolerant of his actions. Our Belladonna baby...

Early on I realized Miley had spay incontinence. It began with drips, but before long it was more. When Cosette developed incontinence we diapered her. At first it was a difficult, humiliating situation for Zette, but she adjusted to her "panties". It would be even harder on Miley to be the only one in diapers, and with a dog door, nearly impossible.

So we handled it differently. I treated her with homeopathic remedies that cut the wet episodes down dramatically. I fed her endocrine system boosting supplements so she would produce the estrogen she needed to keep her bladder valve healthy by way of her glandular system.

We would sometimes go for weeks with no wets. I protected the places she slept with plastic sheeting under the fabric covers. I wrapped my mattress in a shower curtain under the mattress pad. And I washed the dog beds regularly. I became conscious of cleaning products and chemicals since some have an effect on estrogens.

The Providential Doberman

We made little more of it than you would of having a
child who was between diapers and potty training. You
go out to potty on a schedule. You take up the water
after a certain hour. You protect surfaces, and you do a
lot of laundry. I did so much laundry I began making
my own laundry detergent. I named it Miley's Sunshine
Laundry Detergent, and she watched me as I made
every batch...my coach, my mentor. My inspiration.

I love fresh, clean bed linens. Fluffy, lavender-vanilla
scented flannel sheets. Soft, warm fleece sheets and
blankets. And I love new linens. Which is a good thing
because Miss Miles gave me lots of opportunity to buy
new bed linens. It seemed she wanted the bed we
shared made her way, and when I would leave for work
she often gave it a good going over. With her too long
toenails this was not a delicate procedure. By the time
she was done the fitted sheet was often torn. One
afternoon I came home to find the sheet ripped from the
head of the bed to the foot, and all the mattress pad
stuffing all over the room. In the middle of the mess
was a nice soft little nest where my burrowing friend
had spent the day. I wouldn't begin to guess how many
sheets and fleece blankets we went through. Literally
through.

Dobermans have such short hair and thin skin they can feel the textures of the fabrics they come in contact with. And my dogs have always been very opinionated about this. None more so than Miley. When I bought our first set of fleece sheets, stretched them across the feather bed mattress topper, and then invited her to jump up and test them out, I could tell by her reaction that we had just achieved some new level of comfort. She closed her eyes and rubbed her face back and forth across the plush sage green fabric and let out a big sigh. Her mom saw to it that her life was very cushy.

Miley had such a sweet face and friendly demeanor that whenever I took her out in public she would charm all those with whom she came in contact. Multiple times I had people tell me if I ever wanted to part with her to give them a call. I found that amusing. I would just chuckle to myself and think of O'Henry's 1910 short story "The Ransom of Red Chief." In the story, a pair of bumbling criminals kidnap the wealthiest town folks' rowdy son. It didn't take long for the kidnappers of the precocious "Red Chief" to offer money to the boy's parents to take him back! Miley was the embodiment of Red Chief. For most people she would have been a crazy making machine. But she had a *forever*home and that would never change.

It took people with tremendous patience and devotion to tolerate and look beyond Miley's idiosyncrasies. She had been given up on multiple times because of them. Fortunately for all of us, that was not our way. She resided in both our home and our hearts.

Whatever issues Miley had, we patiently dealt with them. We are all products of a combination of elements: genetics, environment, conditioning, and life experience. We can't change the past. But we can overcome some of the damage when we apply unconditional love. When Miley and I met, it was legendary...love at first sight. It needed no explanation, it just was. Non-judgmental acceptance on both our parts. She didn't love me less for my issues and I didn't love her less for hers. And that is what unconditional love is.

Jeanie Notti- Fullerton

Chapter 22

Redesigning Mom

Jeanie Notti- Fullerton

Sometimes a person just has to get real about herself and her life.

I had been working at a non-profit for nearly five years. I had thrown my all into the job, and it left me with very little time or energy for other things. Especially in the summer. And it was affecting my health. My mom was having health problems, too, and needed me for support. My relationship with Marty was suffering. Angus was scheduled for a second major knee surgery. And I longed to spend more time at home with my animals. I was ready for a change.

So in April of 2004, I left my job at the non-profit and went to work at Billy's Organic Food and Lifestyle, a local health food store that was owned by my dear and knowledgeable friend, Carol Larkin. She pulled me lovingly into the beauty of her little store and nurtured me through a rough transition period. I started working only one day a week, which gave me time to heal myself, to become more balanced and centered in a way I hadn't been for several years.

Part of this healing process was spending some meditative time camping. We began this new life by spending a week in the woods. We went to one of our favorite places up the West Fork of the Bitterroot River, where we camped next to a creek, under some tall pine trees in a lush green and grassy part of the forest. The days lengthened into a pleasant spring, moist but not soggy. So we nourished our souls with the gentle warmth of the heightening sun, the rippling sounds of a mountain creek, and crackling campfires under lustrous moonlight.

What we enjoyed the most was watching our beautiful dogs have fun. Their joy of life was contagious. Sophie and Angus would obsess on a raucously scolding chipmunk in a tree for hours, or Sophie would dig a hole sending big plumes of dirt flying that her brother would bite at, filling his face and mouth with the earthy loam. Then they would wade through the creek in the afternoon to cool their feet, after which Sophie would lay in the tall grass on her back sunning her soft, fleshy tummy.

Toots would scratch the pine needles and dirt repeatedly, circling until she had just exactly the correct depression made in the forest floor to really relax in, getting pitch in her glossy black fur so she could take home evidence that she had a great time.

Miley was the only Doberman we've ever had that actually liked to swim. So after she went hunting mice, voles, shrews or whatever rodents were available, and as the day would heat up, she would take a dip in one of the pools at the bends in the creek. She would bound out of the cold water, shake vigorously, and then roll in the grass, scratching her back and scenting herself with nature before drying in the sunbeams sent from heaven just for her. It was as close to paradise as you can get.

In August I took a five day intensive class in equine massage from Coreen Kelly of the Western Montana School of Equine Massage. It was a wonderful experience and easy to translate over into canine massage. I had some posters my friends Mary Wulff and Carol Sanders had given me on the canine musculature system, and I began my own small business -- Tenderheart Animal Massage. It wasn't the most financially prosperous venture I've ever taken on, but I did meet some lovely animals with nice owners. Of course, our dogs were the recipients of my many practice massages.

The summer was spent with at least one camp trip a month and many outings for picnics and barbeques with our dogs. On Labor Day weekend we had a glorious four day campout with our family, Benj and Molly and Caleb-whose-name-means-dog, and their black Labrador, Daisy. By this time Caleb was two and a half years old and more than a little interested in everything. Nature walks were delightful, explaining what things were and how they worked. We enjoyed making S'mores and bug watching, especially the big colorful dragonflies that were flitting in and out of camp. We identified every bird and tree and flower. We watched puffy marshmallow clouds morph into teddy bears and seals and bearded old men. It was obvious that he was going to be an outdoors kid, as both of his parents were outdoorsy. Lots of fishing and camping would be in his future. And hopefully lots of dogs.

It was a sad to see such a weekend come to a close, but life marches on. Though perhaps marching would not be the correct term considering what was about to happen.

Jeanie Notti- Fullerton

Chapter 23

You Reap What You Sow

We were unloading the camper after our wonderful Labor Day campout when I slipped on the metal bottom step and fell off it, turning my ankle. I heard a sickening snapping sound and couldn't breathe or move. When I finally caught my breath, I yelled for help. In the ninety seconds it took for Marty to come out of the house, my foot had swollen so large it was hard to get my slip-on shoe off. I couldn't walk. With his help, I hopped into the house, and he got me an ice pack. Without health insurance I decided to wait it out to see if it got better or if I needed to have it x-rayed. I went straight to bed--the rules are: RICE=rest, ice, compression, elevation. And plenty of homeopathic first aid remedies.

I was now working two days a week at the health food store so I immediately called and found someone else to work for me. I would obviously be laid up for awhile. Marty and I had a nineteen year old girl in transition living with us at the time. JoAnn was a responsible young woman who worked full time, and I trusted her to help out while I was healing. She was especially fond of Angus who had beguiled her into loving him.

I never did have my ankle x-rayed. What appeared to have happened was the tendon snapped off the outside of my ankle and was now riding forward of my ankle bone. I could move it and rotate it with no weight on it,

164

but the ankle was very unstable and I didn't dare walk on it for a couple of weeks. It was crutches and misery. Then a cast-boot borrowed from a friend.

But Miley and Sophie really came through for me. What made it exceptionally good was the way my girls coddled and cuddled with me. Miley would lick my ankle adoringly, trying to salve it with her love. When Miley wasn't licking it Sophie was falling asleep with her head next to or occasionally on my ankle. Toots stayed on a dog bed beside me, and Angus cycled around when the girls would give him room. It was lovely, really. And when the dad was home and there was more opportunity for activity, they worked out a schedule between them. I was never alone for more than a very few minutes. They would take turns being outside, chewing bones, going potty. They saw to it that one of them was on duty at all times. My nursemaids.My best friends.

I've never been good at being inactive. I have to be involved in some mental activity. There I was, in bed, with nowhere to go and nothing to do, surrounded by loving, caring dogs. What could I do? What had I always wanted to do and not had time for? Write poetry and sketch. So for a month I laid on my bed and wrote poem after poem and sketched and taught myself how to draw portraits. Considering the pain I was in, it was some of the best time I've spent!

I had plenty of material to write about just lying there on my bed. I was surrounded by PhD's...Professional house Dogs. It was Miley who inspired the words. I began with "The Providential Doberman" as a poem of love for my little heroine. And from there it grew. Ideas came faster than I could commit them to paper. I had never written poetry before, so if there were rules I didn't know them, and I didn't care. It was all about personal expression.

I did a series of sketches based on sleeping with dogs. All the different positions I woke to find myself in with several dogs in a double bed. Camping in a two man tent with four dogs. The evolution of a dog couch...the couch we had long since lost to them. I laughed as I sketched and wrote and amused myself with my own mental meanderings.

And all the while I was being cared for by the best nurses you could ever hire. All the nights I'd spent sleeping on the floor with ill, injured, or post-surgical dogs were paid back to me by their devoted care when I needed it. I was certainly reaping what I had sown in the way of love and devotion.

My complete healing took several months. It turned out to be healing in a bigger way than just my ankle. I was able to absorb the good energy of my dogs, meditate on the bigger picture of life, and start to focus on what my real dreams and convictions were. The curse of being interested in just about everything is that it is difficult to hone that down and focus on one thing. But after 50 years I finally knew what I wanted to be when I grew up!

Jeanie Notti- Fullerton

Chapter 24

Every Student Needs a Mentor

Jeanie Notti- Fullerton

Homeopathy; the word actually means similar suffering. Based on the science of similars, that which can make ill can also cure when diluted out to just energy. It is energy medicine, quantum physics at its finest. It is safe and sensible.

I realized how important the field of homeopathy had become to me. I had been using homeopathic remedies very effectively on myself, my family and my animals for years, but it was an interest I didn't know enough about. It had a great attraction for me as both a science and an art. So I signed up for a theory class given by a local homeopath. All that did was whet my appetite for more.

I always believed you should exhaust all other possibilities before using a pharmaceutical drug. My philosophy was: Why use a cannon to conquer a problem if a pea shooter is safer, does no peripheral damage, and is equally as effective? Using energy instead of substance made sense to me. I could see it as a way to keep us all healthier, to deal with our day to day injuries and illnesses and to complement all other kinds of treatments.

So I enrolled in the Homeopathy School of Colorado. It was long hours of studying and homework. I was up

170

until all hours of the night, sitting at the computer, or reading by the fire. At first Miley was disconcerted by my not coming to bed with her, and she would check on me regularly trying to persuade me to retire for the night. Sometimes she would just give up and curl up on my feet. I never could stand the idea of her worrying about me, so it was about then I would decide to go to bed.

During my two years of school, the dog children provided me with plenty of injuries and minor illnesses to practice my new skills on! One morning Miley was in serious pain and barely able to walk. I did everything I knew to do. I took her temperature, looked at her gums for capillary recovery time, felt her everywhere, palpated her abdomen. It was obvious she was in some sort of distress, but I couldn't seem to locate exactly what. So we went to see Dr. Hans. He did the same things I did, but then he pushed up from her abdomen and there it was, the pain was in her back. Nothing you could detect from the top side. She had sprained her back somehow, probably roughhousing with Angus. Dr. Hans recommended a muscle relaxant and some Vioxx (just before it was removed from the human market) and a week to ten days of bed rest. I declined the pharmaceuticals, and instead I chose to use homeopathic remedies. Some carefully applied lavender

171

oil as a muscle relaxant and well-chosen homeopathics and Miles was back to herself in three days. We still took it easy with her, but she made a full recovery very quickly. It was good to see that my schooling was paying off for her.

Miley wasn't shy about showing her appreciation. Her rose petal tongue kisses seemed more generously given after any incident that required my acting as nurse to her. This was all the encouragement, the cheering on, the mentoring I needed when I thought I couldn't do it, when I thought I wasn't going to make it through school. I would look at her and all that my care and treatment had done for her and the others and I was heartened to keep going. And on those late nights when I was doing homework right down to the due date, she would come out, and I'd make a bed for her next to me or on my feet. She would patiently wait for me to get done so we could go to bed together. She was the perfect support -- the easel I rested the canvas of my life on as I painted a new picture.

And this is how it went for two years.

Chapter 25

The Big Donnybrook

We often wondered how Angus, the Sean Connery of dogdom, was able to hold his cool and be so patient with Miley. All he ever wanted to do was entertain us with his lolly lips and big, toothy grins. He was born a love sponge, capable of absorbing infinite amounts of affection and attention. He couldn't help that his body grew to be one hundred pounds plus of muscle, bone, and sinew. He was a very big boy in a very small house.

Though Miley really loved Angus, his size was intimidating to her, so their relationship was always on her terms. When she wasn't playing or sharing a sunbeam with the good-natured fellow she would be growling at him, as an alert to where she was and a warning not to step on her. The poor boy, every move he made was scrutinized. He understood her story, but we were concerned about what would happen if he ever lost his patience. And then it happened...

I had just gotten home from a trip to the grocery store; my arms were full of bags as I walked through the back door into the dog room. Yes, we had a dog room built over our back deck. It had a dog door into a large dog yard, a big garden window that allowed plenty of sunbeams to shine on the dog couch, and baskets of toys. It was also our back entry. Normally the three reds were at the door to greet me when I came home, but on this day there was only Sophie.

Then suddenly what sounded like the worst dog fight ever broke out in the kitchen. "**Oh, NO!** He's going to kill her!" was my instant thought. Panic ran through my veins. I dropped the groceries and ran into the house to save her.

As I rounded the corner into the kitchen there they were -- Miley screaming at the top of her lungs while Angus, with his tiny front teeth, had a hold of a teeny little piece of skin on one of her satin cheeks and was pinching and pulling it out about two inches from her face while growling ferociously! Like a really bratty brother pinching a crybaby sister who had been constantly picking on and nagging him. It was really no different than sibling behavior in our own species.

Expecting to see a blood bath, I had gone icy cold and numb with fright. Seeing this was altogether different. I reflexively shouted, "Angus!", but then I had to turn my head away because I couldn't help but laugh. He instantly released his grip and hung his head in embarrassment at getting busted for making his sister cry. He slunk off into the living room.

I immediately looked Miley over well to see if there was any more damage and was pleased to see it was just her satin cheek. The only evidence of the incident was maybe ten missing hairs in a spot about a sixteenth of an inch in diameter. Sophie quickly came behind me and re-examined her.I also checked Angus out to make sure he was alright. He was contrite and apologetic. His patience had just been worn thin.

Naturally, Miley played the part of the classic victim of circumstances to a tee. If Vivian Leigh were alive, she would have been forced to relinquish that *Gone With the Wind* Oscar to Miley. She dramatized it, looking for sympathy wherever she could possibly get it. And Sophie was the perfect person from whom to get it. After casting a disgusted look in Angus' direction, Soph completely ignored her brother while nuzzling and doting on her injured sister. The perceived wound became an object of obsession for Sophie, and she would lie erect with Miley laid out at a ninety degree angle to her, Miles' head draped across her front legs, and she would lick and groom the spot endlessly.

All through our dinner and into the evening, the two of them remained in the same position. At first we mused, "Oh, look at Clara Barton there, nursing the wounded Civil War soldier." Then we realized how long they had been at this. Finally I went over to check on them, and what I saw made me gasp in horror. The whole side of Miley's face was soaking wet, and her adoring sister had licked and groomed a gaping, raw hole the size of a quarter in her satin cheek! What had been nothing was now really something! And both of them were perfectly happy with this situation.

Dr. Mom stepped in at this point with some Schreiner's, a natural liquid with cayenne and goldenseal and other healing substances in it. I swabbed it on the wound and it kept Sophie away from it...for a little while.

The guilt all this gave Angus caused him to divert his eyes and stay close to me for solace. My faith in this gentle giant was intact. I sat on his dog bed with him and stroked his handsome face while telling him how proud I was of him for his patience and tolerance of Miley and her noisy ways. I couldn't get angry with him. For two years he had been putting up with a classic Gloria Swanson drama queen. Other than accidentally stepping on her toe occasionally, he had never hurt her. She, on the other hand, was one minute wanting to romp and play and the next telling him to back off. She was half childhood playmate, half Shakespearean shrew.

Ultimately, it took several weeks for the wound on Miley's cheek to fully heal and grow the hair back. She loved Sophie's ministrations, as a child enjoys a mother's attentions. It was a role Soph was born to play. Angus and Miles made up to each other the next day with nuzzles and a romp, and peace reigned happily ever after.

Chapter 26

When I'm Middle-Aged I Shall Wear Purple

If you read about all the things that can go wrong with a dog breed from their genetic inheritance, and you were a worrier, you would certainly never own a Doberman. They even have a disease named after them, Dancing Doberman Disease. One of the diseases they have a proclivity for is Wobblers Disease, an ailment of the neck that makes them unsteady, wobbly.

We regularly had our veterinarian friend, Dr. Linda Dworak, do cranio-sacral and chiropractic work on each one as injuries or neck and back problems arose. Her work on them was very effective. But after watching a PBS show about Dobermans and seeing what Wobblers does to a dog, I decided to keep the pressure of collars with leashes off their necks. I had also read about a study done on post-mortem dogs' necks and throats and the damage done by collars, and I became determined to protect them against these possibilities.

We decided to invest in harnesses instead. What that meant was three trips to PetSmart in Missoula. In no particularly thought out order, I took Angus first. He came home with a great looking black harness that he seemed a little embarrassed about. But Sophie was fascinated by it, sniffing it all over and watching me carefully as I took it off. Due to the interest she showed, it seemed natural that I would take her next.

It didn't take us very long to choose a pale pink harness that went quite well with Sophie's pink ostrich skin-patterned leather collar. She looked like a million bucks in pink! My kinda girl! When we got home, Angus was delighted to see he wasn't going to be the only one wearing one of these nylon contraptions. Miley, on the other hand, was taken aback. She looked it over as Sophie waltzed into the house to show off the new fashion accessory, but then walked away looking sad and rejected. I gasped. I had no idea she would take something like this so personally. It wasn't like they wore the harnesses 24 hours a day.They were going to wear them occasionally to go to town. But Miley was put last, and it hurt her feelings. I wouldn't have thought she would want a harness at all, but she did because the others each had one. So I didn't wait any longer than necessary to take her to the big city for some serious accoutrement shopping.

When we walked into PetSmart, Miley was eager. She loved the whole experience of walking the aisles and seeing the other animals and getting noticed. When we went down the collar aisle, though, she actually understood why we were there. She began sniffing every one she could reach. I didn't want to have two alike so I looked at all the other colors available. Green and blue were too masculine. So I pulled out purple and a beautiful rainbow color. I liked the rainbow one, even though it was ten dollars more just for the color. It was wonderful next to her pretty milk chocolate colored coat. However, the choice was hers. She sniffed them over and then gave the nod to the purple one. I questioned it, but she was sure of her decision. So I put it on her, adjusted it up, snapped the leash on, and she wore it to the cash register to pay for it. It was not my first choice of colors, but it was the one she liked, the one that resonated with her. It was a royal color for a princess. And she made it beautiful. Her decision made me smile.

When we got home, she came in the house as proud as if it had been diamond studded. She bounced and jumped around and made sure everyone admired it. Once again, there was so much appreciation for such a little thing. It filled my cup to overflowing with gratitude for her.

Chapter 27

Twisted

Sunday, April 8th, 2007. I had been up most of the night with some sort of gastro-intestinal upset. Not feeling well, I stayed home from our spiritual meeting that afternoon. It was a gorgeous spring day, and I had puttered around in my vegetable garden a little that morning. We were preparing to build a new deck on the front of our house, and we had a set of temporary steps at the front door. They were ugly, and I decided to set a large resin rabbit on the top step to distract from them. We so rarely used the front door it hardly seemed like it mattered.

At 2:30 I decided it would be a really good thing for my health to take a little nap. The covered swing was set up in the front yard, and the sun was inviting me to come out and bask in it. So I headed out the front door. Just as I stepped out onto the top step, all the dogs rushed the door. I knew better than this! The dogs seemed to feel it was their personal duty to rush out the door barking ahead of me to clear the yard of any riff raff. I was their charge, and they were my bodyguards and they took the job seriously. When I wanted to go outside without the fanfare, I had to stop them at the door, ask them to sit and stay so I could walk out in peace, and then release them. I suppose because I wasn't feeling well, I wasn't thinking as clearly as I could have been.

As my beautiful dog pack rushed out the front door, they knocked me off balance. I fell, from a height of about forty inches, to the ground, onto the point of my right shoulder, and my right leg twisted -- and folded right over the top of the resin rabbit. The sound of the snap was beyond sickening. It was the sound of breaking a good sized dry branch before tossing it onto the campfire. Only more violent.

I knew in the nano-second it took me to hit the ground, I was in deep trouble. When I sat up and looked at my leg, my foot was twisted in an entirely different direction than my knee indicated it should be. And I was home alone.

Okay...when presented with a situation like this, you have to do whatever you can. I could lie there and go into shock waiting for Marty to get home and find me, or I could try to get myself in the house and deal with this. The first choice didn't really occur to me until months later. I knew immediately I had to get myself back into the house, to the phone, and call for help. Thankfully, and by some miracle, my head had missed a large rock by only a couple of inches and my shoulder was not broken. I was able to move myself and to crawl, though there was no way to stand. There were five steps on the stairs...if I wanted help I would have to brave it and crawl up, letting my foot just flop against each step on the way. So that's what I did. At the second to the top step I was able to reach the door handle and open the screen door and crawl through.

My homeopathy kit was across the living room, close to the phone, so I dragged myself to it and immediately took a dose of each high potency aconite and arnica. I grabbed the phone and crawled to the kitchen. I was grateful for a small house and a bottom mount freezer. I got out a five pound bag of Costco frozen green beans, lay on my side so I could line my foot up with my leg, and put the icy bag o' beans on my badly broken leg. Then I dialed the hall where my family was attending the meeting which had just gotten over. A friend answered the phone and said Marty was gone but Benj and Molly were just getting in their car. He ran out and caught them, and they came as fast as four-way flashers would allow them to go.

Meanwhile my dogs knew there was trouble...big trouble. I had a handle instead of a knob put on our back door, and then we taught Sophie and Angus how to use it so they would never get left outside accidentally. They knew how to push it down with one fell swoop and walk in. They must have really been stressed because I could hear them whining and barking and crying and digging at the door handle but not opening the door. It took them several minutes to conquer something that took them about three seconds normally. All the while Sophie must have had her paw on the doorbell because it kept ringing repeatedly.

When they finally got in the house, my darling Sophie, my own Florence Nightingale, ran in -- and sat on me. I screamed. She ran. I never saw the others. I was fairly certain, though, that Angus was standing guard at the door, and he would never have allowed paramedics in our house even if it was to help me. He knew his job.

I took some more homeopathics. They reduced the pain to virtually nothing so long as I was still, and I didn't feel shocky at all. I was grateful for that; I didn't want to pass out or to not be in charge of what may be about to happen to me. I needed to be my own best health advocate especially since I had no health insurance.I wanted no panic driven procedures.

When Benj and Molly arrived, he ran around and found materials to splint my twisted leg: a greasy cardboard car parts box from his dad's garage, a dirty sheet from the laundry, and some duct tape. I was never as proud of one of my son's art projects as I was of this one! Molly brought my hair and tooth brushes to me for some quick grooming. When Marty arrived, they loaded me in the back of the Explorer and away we went to the hospital. I would be there four days, and the stay would include surgery to install a steel rod in the severe spiral break.

I wondered how the dogs were taking my absence. Marty said they were very quiet, depressed. Benj said when they arrived at the house, Miley was hiding under my computer desk. This was the same thing she did the evening we had an earthquake. She apparently could feel the build-up to the quake, and she went under the dining room table and wouldn't come out. As soon as the earthquake passed, she came out and we agreed the next time she went under something we would pay attention. My little seismograph friend knew this was a catastrophe.

When I came home, it was in a wheelchair. They said I would be in it for four months. Our house is too small for a wheelchair, and it couldn't round the hallway corner into the bedroom, so a walker became helpful.

From the instant we got home, Miley was my constant companion. She had been sleeping with me for over four years and she knew how to sleep at my feet without crowding, so I welcomed her back into bed with me.

The others were entirely intimidated. I smelled very unusual, not like anything they had ever experienced.I understood. I needed to apologize to Sophie for screaming when she sat on me. I'm sure in her mind she was there to protect me as best she could under the circumstances, and I rejected her help. Sophie is as sensitive as she is beautiful, and she was hurt, too. Angus and Toots just hung back, afraid to hurt me again.

Miley, however, was a rock. Even to eat, drink and go potty she only left me for a few minutes at a time. Once again she would be my best friend, my nurse, lying next to my broken leg and emitting warmth and energy that would promote fast healing and get me out of the wheelchair in two months -- half the time they predicted. She was homeopathic to my leg, to my life.

For the next several months, I spent much of my time in bed, healing. Miley and I watched out the big bedroom window as the trees leafed out and the weather warmed. We watched as the birds found mates and made nests and raised their young, as the lilacs and climbing roses bloomed and faded. We enjoyed having some visitors, and we appreciated our alone time, too. We were old friends who could be content in each other's presence with or without talking.

Sophie eventually joined us on the bed, though without as good judgment as Miley, she jumped up on my broken leg a time or two and got in trouble for that. Since I didn't have a cast, my leg was largely unprotected from being bumped and battered. Miley once again licked and nurtured the injury.

The break came at an interesting time...the last quarter of my homeopathy schooling. In less than two months I would be required to take my final exam. Meanwhile I had final homework assignments and some intense studying to do. For the first two weeks after the break my concentration was compromised by pain medication. But as I weaned off of that and was taking just homeopathics my thoughts cleared, allowing me to really hit the books.

I had my final exam proctored by NansuRoddy at our local library, and I took the four hour test in the wheelchair. Miley and Sophie waited in the car while Marty ran errands and I worked my way through the exam. I could look out the library window and see my cheerleading team was there for me on the sidelines. I was thrilled to have made it to the end of the four part test without much physical discomfort. I passed finals with a high score and was officially a certified homeopath. Though I needed to heal myself before I could ply my science/art.

As the summer wore on and I continued to heal, I decided to take up another project:a book of wisdom and life lessons for my darling grandson, Caleb-whose-name-means-dog. I told him the stories of his history, of his family's history, of my love for dogs and animals of all sorts. I told him my thoughts on love, beauty, and bravery. I gifted him with my secret recipes. And I gave him the words of others;so many people with so much wisdom to quote - Jesus Christ, Gandhi, Mother Theresa, Albert Einstein, Henry Ford, Mark Twain...and dozens of others. I filled three hundred sixty two handwritten pages of a leather bound journal and then transcribed them to the computer. It was a labor of love.

All of which was done with Miley at my side, inspiring the words, encouraging me to continue writing while I was healing.

Jeanie Notti- Fullerton

Chapter 28

The Sous Chef

As I healed and life became more normal once again, I found even more pleasure in the things I hadn't been able to do for months. Things like cooking for the dogs. For awhile I was only able to coach Marty or my lovely niece, Cheri, who came to take care of us all when my leg was broken, on how to make their food. It was a joy to be able to care for them again myself. I was the one who put the energy of love into it.

I have always enjoyed cooking (it's my Italian heritage)…but I'm an admittedly messy cook and it's the clean-up I don't care for. Even so, I was now infused with enthusiasm for making beautiful and delicious food for all of us. I spent time developing recipes of my own and working them out in the kitchen. All the while I had one helper, my sous chef, Miley. If something hit the floor I would call out "Clean up in aisle five!", and she was right there to lap up the mess. She got to taste many delicacies just because she hung out with me. Pot and pan and plate licking was evenly divided, but since Miley was always in the kitchen she was the one who got the test bites. And she often snatched the stirring spoon off the counter to lick it. She wasn't going to let anything go to waste.

I can't say Miles had particularly refined taste buds. She was as discriminating as the typical Doberman, as likely to enjoy catching and eating a fly as she was happy for a bite of a perfectly barbecued marinated tri-tip steak or rich, creamy huckleberry cheesecake. They all enjoyed grazing on horse manure first thing in the morning. So much so we began calling it "The Breakfast of Champions." It seemed to me their need for "greens" went right along with the popularity of wheat grass and other green products in the health food industry. They were health trendsetters. But it was Miley's vocal, whole hearted excitement and displays of appreciation for food that set her apart.

My dear friend Mary (Mary Wulff, herbalist and co-author of Herbs for Pets) and I had been so impassioned about feeding dogs we began teaching Canine Cuisine classes. We'd done our research, and between the two of us had many years of experience to share. We believe what Hippocrates said, "Let food be your medicine," applies to dogs, too. How can anyone stay healthy if they get one bowl of dry cereal a day? Dogs are omnivores, eating all sorts of foods, but they are primarily carnivores. They need to have protein in the form of meat to stay at their optimum health. That is how they were created. They have a short and efficient digestive system that is well designed for breaking down whole foods.

There is an intelligence in the way wild dogs eat prey. They commonly eat the gut of the animal first. With eighty percent of our immune response dependent on the health of the intestinal tract, this is innately wise. That is where all the digestive enzymes and probiotics are that help the meal to break down. Any grains and seeds they eat are contained in the gut, semi or predigested. We need to take a clue from that. And within the prey animal there is the right mix of organ and muscle meat and bone to balance the diet.

These are the things needed to keep a dog healthy. Mary and I focused our classes on these basic principles plus the avoidance of toxins, the addition of some supplements, and having fun with the concept. We even served homemade dog cookies as refreshments to show our students that it's all good. Smiley Miley's Ginger Hearts...delicious.And Angus' Blueberry Stud Muffins.Mmmm, good. Our hope was that other dogs got to eat well and be healthier, happier, and more energetic because of Mary and my willingness to share what we had learned. We worked to make it easier for their owners to transition them into a balanced holistically made food by way of our support.

Of course our dogs enjoyed eating. I rotated the types of meat I used and chose the vegetables according to the season. I learned to germinate grain to increase the nutritional factors. All because it is better for them to eat real whole foods than to eat manufactured dry food.

I used an old horseman's technique for slowing my enthusiastic diners down as they ate so they would never experience bloat. I found a couple of nice big smooth rocks (too big to bite or mouth in any way), and I laid them on top of their food before I gave it to them. They had to roll the rocks around or flip them out of their bowls in order to get to all their food, and it slowed them down so they could actually taste their wholesome homemade victuals. Now they make bowls with big bumps in them to do the same thing, but the rocks worked for us.

Miley's enthusiasm for being my sous chef was natural. Between the sights, the smells, and the flavors it was a canine culinary paradise in my kitchen once a week as I stirred up thirty five to forty pounds of fresh homemade provisions. I talked to her the entire time I was cooking, because she was interested in everything I did. And a good sous chef is hard to find...

Jeanie Notti- Fullerton

Chapter 29

Dr. Dog

As my homeopathic practice grew Miley and Sophie became very important to both me and my patients. I always knew Sophie wanted to be a healer, but Miley was equally as adept at seeing into the souls of the walking wounded and doing the appropriate thing to help.

One patient in particular was outstanding. She did not like dogs, not having ever been around dogs she was afraid of them. In consideration of that I shut the dogs out of my home office while I took the case. Miley, with her persistent need to be with me, had a major meltdown and could be heard from the dog room crying and scratching madly at the door. Usually the canine kids would settle down after a few minutes of separation; after all they were only thirty feet away, safe in their dog room with all the amenities dogs could ever want and some they hadn't thought of. But not on this day. Finally I asked my patient if she would mind my letting just this one dog in so we could quell the noise. She hesitantly agreed.

After Miley greeted me enthusiastically, she went and sat by the woman. She didn't nudge her as she usually would when begging for attention. She just sat there quietly next to the patient, not even looking at her consistently. After a few minutes the woman reached out and touched her. Miley stayed still.

Over the course of the next hour I observed the woman visibly relax as she stroked Miley's satin face, head, and neck. She told her story completely, feeling the energy of a place that was safe. I was awed at the healing power this dog emitted once again. And at the power of quiet.

Before the woman left, she paused, and, with her hand on Miley's head, said, "She's so sweet." No truer words were ever spoken.

For every kindness I had ever extended to her, Miley repaid me a thousand-fold by being by my side and watching over me. We both knew pain and shared it. And in the sharing there was strength. And compassion.And success. We were partners in every endeavor, whether it was cooking or camping or going to school or healing others. We looked out for each other in an unspoken agreement that was as natural as breathing. We experienced life together on the same plane and we were both better for it.

Jeanie Notti- Fullerton

Chapter 30

And We All Lived Happily Ever After

Loved, well cared for, pampered, spoiled, appreciated for whom she was and what she brought to our family, Miley had a fabulous life with us. She filled our lives with fun and noise, enthusiasm and joy. As with all of us, she was imperfect, but, like beauty, perfection may be in the eyes of the beholder. She was *absolutely perfect* for the job she was sent to do.

As life comes and goes on this planet, we are forced to try to find a way to make sense of it all. Like most humans, I find the more I learn the more I realize how little I know. There is one thing I'm absolutely certain of though -- I have experienced giving and receiving unconditional love at its finest. Miley's and my love for one another was as pure as love gets. Epic.Legendary. And love never fails.

To the last instant of this life we lived happily ever after.

For some who may read this book, this is where the story needs to end. With an everlasting love whose energy will continue to brighten the world for eternity. For you the final chapter is 33 -- The Lessons Live On.

For others, there is the rest of the story, that of the finality of life. With my blessing, you may choose for yourself where you would like this tale to end for you.

Chapter 31

Love Never Fails

Marty got home from work on Monday, September 29th, 2008, to find Miley ill. He called me at work, and I told him to rush her to Dr. Hans, and I would meet them there.

Marty said she was near to collapse when he got home. I was shocked to see her. This was not the same dog I had kissed goodbye that morning.Dr. Hans checked her over completely, drew blood, and I took the sample to the hospital laboratory so we could get the test results early the next morning. Miley was obviously very ill. Hans said her heartbeat was very faint. And he suggested we have an ultrasound done of her heart and abdomen the next day.

We took her home and pampered her all evening. She was disinterested in food but ate a few bites to please me. I gave her several homeopathics until she finally perked up. We slept fitfully on a dog bed with her under the pretty new rose patterned woobie we had just purchased for her two days before.

The next morning I collected a urine sample from her to take to the vet clinic. I convinced myself that this couldn't be anything too serious. Perhaps her thyroid was very low. If she did have a heart problem there are a lot of homeopathics and supplements and herbs besides the conventional medicines that treat heart conditions. We could deal with this. Maybe she had an infection that we'd missed...

Hans called me at 8:30 a.m. to let me know her blood test was all perfectly normal except for a little anemia. See, I told myself, it just couldn't be anything too serious... But he insisted we shouldn't overlook anything and said he would call the clinic in Missoula immediately to order an ultrasound as soon as possible. I called to set up the appointment for 2:30 that afternoon. Mary said she would go with us.

I was blindsided. The sonogram revealed advanced hemangio-sarcoma...an aggressive blood borne cancer. It was on her spleen and had metastasized to several places. Her illness was from one of the blood-blister-like tumors bursting and the internal bleeding it caused. This was why her heartbeat was so faint. It was all the fluid. The veterinarian said there was nothing that could be done for her. The prognosis was minutes, hours, days...

I gasped. I felt Mary's arm around my shoulder. As soon as Miley was safely on the floor, I crumpled and just sat there and sobbed. I could barely breathe, and I was instantly numb all over. Mary took Miles outside while I struggled to compose myself enough to pay the bill.

Mary drove home as I couldn't stop crying. How could this have happened??? What did I miss??? Miley had some days during the summer that she was lethargic, tired. But it was often when it was hot and she never liked heat. There was never anything I could put my finger on. No vomiting, no diarrhea, no fever. No loss of appetite. She slept next to me always, even allowing me to cuddle her more often. She was my sous chef. My best friend. I'm in the healing arts, *how could I have missed this in someone I loved so much???*

I was devastated. I couldn't catch my breath. Marty was standing in the yard waiting for us when we got home. He opened the back car door and just burst into a cascade of uncontrollable tears when Miley got out. Our baby, our little princess. Minutes, hours, days... *How could this be???*

We were in shock, and neither of us could stop crying. We had been upset by her illness, but hopeful, positive. In our minds, at nine and a half years old she still had a lot of years left with us. She had only been our dog-child for five years and nine months. Not long enough. Eternity would not have been long enough.

We'd had a great summer. We'd gone on a couple of good camping trips. Miley had so much fun. She ran and dug holes and fell into an unexpectedly deep pool of water when she went to go wading. She got silly and made us laugh as she shook off and raced around to dry out. She had spent countless hours mousing in the front field, lying on the lawn watching me garden, rolling in the soft grass to scratch her back, digging in my flower bed. We'd had barbeques on our big new deck. She'd licked a lot of plates, pots and pans. She even went to get firewood with her dad one day. We had lived life to the full. We were so happy.

That night, we decided to make beds on the living room floor and treat it like a big doggie slumber party. We didn't want her to exert herself by jumping on the bed. Hemangio-sarcoma is an aggressive cancer, quick spreading. Exertion can cause the tumors to burst. And that can be fatal.

We didn't sleep much that night. All we could do was watch our Miley and reflect on how good our lives were with her. I gave her homeopathic remedies to keep her comfortable and we took some to calm our sorrow.

Marty took the next day off. He couldn't bear to leave Miley. We went to the health food store to get some herbal cancer fighting agents and immune system boosters for her. And we took her to lunch at McDonald's. I changed her diet to the cancer fighting diet, with no carbohydrates whatsoever, just meat and vegetables and essential fatty acids. My dear friend, Vicki Allsop, came to our home and did some hands-on energy work on Miley that afternoon. After a few minutes of working with Miles, Vicki asked me if I was ready to say goodbye. "I'll **never** be ready to say goodbye to her..." **Ever...**

The Thursday after the diagnosis I told Miley we had to stop crying all the time. We were living as though we were dying. We had to begin living for the minute, for the hour, for the day. From that moment on I relished her episodes of barking at the window even though I knew the energy she put into her theatrics had the potential of causing a bleed. She needed to be herself. There needed to be joy and interest. After all, she was still alive! My Miley was still with me!

We had more good days than bad days, and the bad days were actually only a couple of hour stretches in the day. Then Miles would rally and we would have good quality again. We were all coping, living for the joy of each good moment.

One morning, however, Marty awoke to Toots having a bad spell. Like a seizure, she was barely able to walk and then she would collapse. She'd had two episodes before, and she recovered quickly with homeopathic treatment. Hans had checked her out both times and found nothing wrong, but an MRI might reveal something more serious in her brain, though there wouldn't be anything that could be done. The stress of it all was too much for Marty to deal with altogether, and he thought it must be time for fifteen year old Toots to go. He was thinking of taking her in to be euthanized that day so she wouldn't suffer. He asked me to call Hans and tell him what was going on. I treated Toots with some appropriate homeopathic remedies throughout the day and she rallied.

Our patient and dear veterinarian listened to me sob and babble about this being too much for us to bear. How did we know when time was at its end? How do we determine what suffering is? He sent us a Quality of Life evaluation form via email to help us deal with our feelings. It was truly a blessing. With it we realized that both Miley and Toots were having a good quality of life even though both were having some troubles. It reassured Marty that Toots was not suffering. By late afternoon he could see she had come through the episode.

There was someone with Miley every second. We had her "Aunt" Mary stay with her for three hours one day when our schedules required both of us to be gone. I was frantic for those three hours, sick to my stomach that I had to leave her. But her Aunty loved her and took good care of her while we were gone.

We all continued to sleep on dog beds in the living room. Isn't this where this life began? She kept her pretty woobie near her at all times. She couldn't eat big meals anymore so I fed her small amounts several times a day. It was such a joy to feed her. I hand fed her from a fork. My baby...

Then one night twelve days after this began things took a turn for the worse and we realized it was coming to an end. Miley's breathing was labored. She looked ill. She couldn't sleep. She could barely walk across the room before she would have to lie down and rest. I woke Marty up at 2:30 a.m. and told him if she made it through the night we would have to make one of the worst decisions of our lives in the morning. We laid on the floor on either side of her and prayed and talked to her and told her of our great love for her. We told her how blessed we were that some angel-who-loves-dogs brought her to us, and that she wanted to live with us.

She reached out and gave each of us a rose petal tongued kiss. The last ones.

At 8 a.m. I called Hans and told him we needed his help. We met him and Mary at the clinic at 9:30. And then it was over. This final act of love. Or so they say. I held Miley close and kissed her and told her I loved her so as she let go of life. And a part of me died right there with her.

Jeanie Notti- Fullerton

Chapter 32

The Work of Grieving

Sunday morning...I slept only minutes at a time during the night. I woke regularly sobbing for my lost baby. The house was so quiet it was deafening. The change in the energy was horrid. As if the electricity had gone out. There didn't seem to be enough energy in the house to make any one of us function. How could one little red waif have brought so much light into our lives? Everything in the house had absorbed her joy of living and now it was all fading.

How could you leave me, Miley? How will I ever live with this hole in my soul that *only you* could fill? How can a heart this broken keep on beating? What just happened to the big family we had always wanted? How can I ever describe this kind of grief? Words are so inadequate, but Kahlil Gibran said it best: "And ever it has been that love knows not its own depth until the hour of separation."

Could there ever possibly be anything sadder than an empty dog collar? I ache for the feel of Miley's sturdy little body in my arms. I rode so many miles in the truck with her laid across my lap, my arms wrapped around her stroking her body. The first ride in the truck after she was gone I sobbed because I didn't know what to do with my arms and hands.

All my weaknesses are exposed like Job's ulcers. My faith is rattled. I sincerely believe Miley came to me via Providence, from a benevolent God, by way of an angel-who-loves-dogs. Marty and I have a strong belief system based on the Bible. One that guarantees a resurrection for mankind. Yet there doesn't seem to be the same *written* contract for animals. They are our wards, and we are to take care of them. They feed, clothe and work for us. They are our companions, our servants, our entertainment, and they make the world an infinitely more interesting place. Could it be that God has a contract with them, too, but theirs is written on their hearts instead of in a book?

Jesus pointed to the sparrows as considered by men of very little value. Yet, he said, his Father knows when a sparrow falls **and remembers** (Matthew 10:28-30 & Luke 12:5-7). Certainly if He remembers a sparrow, He will remember someone so dynamic as Miley. He knows they give us everything they have, these dogs of ours, and in return we just give our leftovers...our leftover time, leftover energy, leftover food...

It is stated "The righteous one is caring for the soul of his domestic animal." (Proverbs 12:10). I pray God will see our loving kindness toward those fallen animals, which He hasn't forgotten, and judge us with the same benevolence.

Usually men and women mourn differently. Sometimes that difference can destroy their relationship. Marty and I have experienced some of that in the past. But with each successive loss we have learned to draw closer, to mourn more alike. I am still more open, more vocal, more incapacitated by the loss, but he also suffers aloud. He has cried openly more for Miley than any other time. We are equally as exhausted by the grief. But as the waves come and go for me, he has learned to just quietly be near, not to run and hide or be artificially comforting. When I had the last film of Miley developed, we sat and looked at the photos together and we both wept.

Of course, there are people who don't understand and whose comments reflect a lack of empathy. I feel sad for them. Perhaps they have never felt a love as deeply as this and lost it. It is a blessing to have loved someone else *more* than you love yourself.

The other dogs are very comforting. They never leave my side. If I get up and walk across the room, so do they. They are mourning, too. Sophie has lost her playmate, and she is sad. Toots is needy, worried. Perhaps she feels her own mortality. Angus has chewed all the hair off his flanks in the last few weeks; he's been anxious. He sleeps close to me. But I can tell by the weight of the blanket that it isn't Miley at the end of the bed. I cry myself to sleep every night and awaken crying every morning. My sorrow is for their loss as well as my own.

The quiet is gut wrenching. Miley was the one who got everyone moving, playing, excited about every outside movement. Without her it is oppressively silent.

Tuesday Mary stopped by the health food store to see if I was okay on my first day back at work. Then she handed me a beautifully wrapped box. When I opened it there was an exquisite set of copper with amber wind chimes … to bring the noise back. It was the most thoughtful tribute to who Miley was. My friends Jean and Jack Atthowe gifted us with a beautiful mauve colored river rock with **Miley** carved into it to memorialize our girl. Trista brought roses…and roses…and more roses. There were donations made in Miley's name to the Montana Companion Animal Network and to the Bitter Root Humane Association and Rolling Dog Ranch. And there were beautiful cards. All of it is in a collection alongside her ashes. It is all so precious to me right now.

One morning I had a dream that I woke to something stirring at the end of the bed. I looked up and there was an old quilt top from one of Benj's baby blankets lying on the bed. Something whined underneath it. I sat up and lifted the quilt and there she was! *My Miley!!* She was so beautiful I gasped. Her coat had grown in thick and dark and like silk velvet. There were no scars anywhere. Her little feet were kitty paws, as they should be. I could see in her face she was overjoyed to see me. And all I could say was, "Oh, Miley! You're so beautiful! I couldn't do that for you. Only God could do that." At that moment I awoke, sobbing. I had seen her so clearly. Please, dear God, make it so.

You hardly ever grieve just the incident of the moment. You find that all the losses you've had in the past are suddenly fresh again. This one is the rawest, but the others are there, too. I have many regrets, and I bludgeon myself with them. I question every action I've ever taken, every decision I've ever made. Eventually I have to learn to accept all that has happened, not so much because I want to but because I have no choice.

And I miss them all again: the dogs of my youth, Cappy, Tawny, and Spike. The dogs of my adulthood: adorable Sookie, the independent Beagle-Bassett hound. My precious Messina, my first Doberman and the one who saved Benj's life. Sweet Lady Anne the quiet, shy German Shepherd-Husky. Beloved Cosette.Now Miley Anne. I miss all the horses, Flipper, BeeBee, Babe, Star, Tuco, Pete, Macho, Sunny. And the cats, Penelope, Max, Tig, Gatsby, Sasha, Fantasy, and Duchess. I miss the sheep and the chickens. I miss the guinea pigs, the parakeets, the goose, the pigeon, the turtle, and the fish. I even miss animals that weren't mine. My Dad's Joe, Benj and Molly's Buck,Nadine's Rosy,Sally's Betsy and Phoenix, Peggy's Summer,Pam's horses Spence and Louie, and Mary's Cedar.

I don't know how I will survive the loss of the others. I don't know how I've survived the ones I've lost thus far. When Cosette died I wanted to go with her. Wherever her energy was, I wanted to be there, too. So I had her cremated, that someday our ashes may be together forever. Miley now joins her. And someday I will join them.

I ache inside and there is a weight like a cinder block in my chest. People make mistakes. I have made plenty. I have deep regrets about the dogs I've had in the past when I didn't know what I know now. I have guilt for my lack of thoughtfulness in their care and keeping. I pray to be forgiven for that.

Maya Angelou once said, "You did what you knew to do, and when you knew better you did better." I am comforted by that thought. But there is a mourning for not knowing more, sooner, a heaviness of heart for my own ignorance and the suffering that may have caused.

It's been six weeks and I still sob every day, multiple times in the day. Everything reminds me of Miley. When I reach into the bag for dog cookies my hand automatically brings out four. I cry as I put one back. We've found old woobies here and there. A scrap of one was under the recliner. Another was in my closet. Her nose prints are still on the glass of the front door...I can't wash them away. I pulled the couch out to vacuum and there was her missing hollow bone that we would stuff with peanut butter. There is no one waiting in the driveway to give me rose petal tongue kisses when I get home. I will never see Miley with her kitty friend Mewsette sitting together on the top of the haystack again. I look for her every time I drop some little morsel of food in the kitchen. My stirring spoons are never disturbed when I leave them on the counter. I couldn't put her little stainless steel dinner dish away, so I now use it as my popcorn bowl though she is no longer here to catch the kernels. And it is so miserably quiet.

Just a week after Cosette died I was holding her dog collar and crying when I realized how much I loved her dog tag. It was not just a stainless steel circle; there was also a brass heart with it. She was such a girly-girl, actually enjoying having her nails polished and a pearl cabochon glued to her pretty ear. Her tag was more a pendant than a dog tag. So I took it off her collar and hung it on a box chain around my neck. In over seven years I'd had it off for only the three hours that I was in surgery to mend my broken leg. During that time Marty was to keep it warm and safe in his breast pocket, over his heart. The minute I was back in my room he was to put it back on my neck...and he did.

Now I needed something from Miley to have and to hold with me for the rest of my life, and I only had a brass plate on her collar. So I went to a local jewelry store to see what I might find that would represent my dearest friend. What I found was so perfect, so exquisite...a 14K white gold charm, a large open heart with a smaller open heart linked into it. Hearts entwined...a mama heart and a baby heart. It is the ultimate expression of Miles and my love. It will be with me to the end.

As good as it gets in this world is to be loved exquisitely, unconditionally, just for who you are.

Jeanie Notti- Fullerton

Chapter 33

The Lessons Live On

Three weeks after losing Miley, Marty and I were at a large chain store when we somehow got separated. I walked all over the store and couldn't find him. At first I was upset and annoyed by the situation. And then I thought of Miley. I went back to the place I saw him last, patiently waited, and within five minutes he showed up. It was the lesson I learned from my street smart Miley. Perfect logic.

My Miley was one of a kind. Lucky? -- Yes, she was ultimately very lucky. She was blessed to journey to me. But we were more blessed to have her touch our lives so deeply. I will never be the same. I'll be forever grateful to God and to the angel-who-loves-dogs that brought her to my open arms, because I had so much to learn.

I learned about how families work. How love multiplies on itself. I learned to trust my instincts, my intuition. I learned to listen when Providence speaks.

I learned that an internal sense of safety and security is not always dependent on another person protecting you. Instead it is the confidence you feel when you know someone loves you with their whole heart. It is a state of mind, an attitude of self-assurance, which keeps you mindful and therefore safe. I learned that to face down a dragon for what you want, for what you believe in, will make you strong.

I learned that forgiveness of others is the greatest gift you can give yourself, not holding on to grievances, and that when you can forgive you are able to move on, completely free.

I learned how important it is for your name to be safe in someone's mouth.

I learned that exuberance should never be squelched. I learned that all you need to do to be a comfort to a friend is be there. I learned that to communicate with another species all you have to do is listen with an open heart. I learned that when you give to a rescue dog you get back a thousand times more than you could ever give.

I learned that to love unconditionally is to see with your heart and not with your eyes. I learned not to be quick to judge, as the surface looks and actions are not always an accurate reflection of the heart of someone.

I learned that being united in purpose makes for a strong marriage. I learned that when you take someone for better and for worse, the 'worse' can be a time for

personal analysis and growth if you allow it to be.
I learned never to say never because that closes the door
to miracles. I learned to be grateful for the unexpected.

I learned that without faith there is nothing; that faith is,
as Hebrews 11:1 says, "the assured expectation of things
hoped for, the evident demonstration of realities though
not yet beheld."

And I've learned so much more. All because I opened
my heart to a little red dog that needed me, and then
realized that I needed her just as much. Without testing
it, how can you know how much your heart can hold?
As it turns out, there is no limit.

I knew from the moment I met Miley that there was a
story to be told, a book to be written. The 19th century
book "Beautiful Joe" by Margaret Marshall Saunders
had a deep and profound effect on me as a child...and
then 40 years later there she was...my very own
Beautiful Joe, sent to me for a purpose. I was born to
write this book...life coming full circle.

My hope and dream is that this writing will encourage
even just one person to consider a rescue dog. The love
and appreciation received from someone whose life is so
tenuous, future so uncertain, is beyond description.

There are no words adequate to express the feelings. Your self-esteem is automatically improved just by the fact that you did the right thing. You find that it is they who rescue you. If out of nothing else but mediocrity.

If just one heart is touched, if just one dog is given a forever home, loved and cherished like Miley because of all these words, her joy and her work for me and for the world will be complete.

Jeanie Notti- Fullerton

"Do not forget hospitality, for through it some, unknown to themselves, entertained angels."

--Hebrews 13:2

Amen and amen.

<u>Smiley Miley's Ginger Hearts</u>

½ c. molasses

2 T. Agave Syrup or honey

¼ c. water

1 lg. egg

¼ c. oil

Mix together. Fold in:

3 ½ c. flour (½ oat flour, ½ rice flour)

1 ½ T. xanthum gum

1 t. baking soda

1 ¼ t. cinnamon

½ t. cloves

2 T. ginger

¼ c. chopped pecans or almonds

Roll ¼" thick on floured surface. Cut out with a heart shaped cookie cutter. Bake 15 minutes at 350 degrees.

<u>Miley's Sunshine Laundry Detergent</u>

6 cups water

1/2 bar Fels-Naptha soap, grated

1 cup Arm & Hammer Super <u>Washing</u> Soda (not baking soda)

1 cup 20 Mule Team Borax

Mix Fels-Naptha soap in a saucepan with 6 cups hot water, and heat on low until dissolved. Stir in Arm & Hammer Super Washing Soda and 20 Mule Team Borax. Stir until thickened (about 20 minutes) and remove from heat.

Put 1 quart hot water into a 2-gallon bucket. Add soap mixture, and mix well.

Fill bucket with additional 3 ½ quarts of hot water and mix well.

Set aside for 24 hours or until mixture thickens. Use 1/2 cup of mixture per regular sized load.

Makes 1.5 gal.

Gratitude andAcknowledgements

I have so much to be grateful for, it's hard to know where to start. So I think I'll try to do this in order. 'In the beginning'...

I thank Jehovah God for creating all the animals. And that, in His wisdom and love, He created the domestic animals especially for man's enjoyment and companionship. He gave them qualities we aspire to, such as pure unconditional love, loyalty, patience, long-suffering, humility, devotion, selflessness, and so much more. He told us to look to them as our teachers. It requires humbling oneself to recognize the lessons of the animal world...and God loves the humble. I thank Him for the way Miley providentially came to me.

I thank my parents, John and Colleen Notti, for loving me enough to take it seriously when my first words were 'Mama', 'Dada', 'horsey'. When I rode a Wonder Horse until its head fell off, they knew I wasn't going to stop loving horses, or, for that matter, animals in general. They moved us to the country and I've never been without animals since. It was wonderful to grow up with lots of pets, including dozens of roly-poly yellow Labrador puppies, and leggy foals, and fuzzy kittens, and all their lovely parents. They were all my teachers, my friends, my family. I'm very grateful my parents made the decision to raise me as a country girl.

I also thank my Mom for her support in my professional career choice to be a homeopath. It took a long time for me to figure out what I wanted to be when I grew up! We have seen homeopathy work in our lives, and we are all better for it, both people and animals. It was a gift to us all.

I thank Marty, a city boy who quickly adapted to country life. When he proposed to me, my first words were, "I come with two horses. If you can accept that, the answer is yes." It was a long term commitment in so many ways. Not many people can say they've had a horse for thirty years, from birth to death. I've had two. I've been blessed. Marty has learned to be a hobby farmer, changing sprinkler pipes and stacking hay. He's been bucked off horses repeatedly, and he's never held it against the horse. He's a great dog and cat dad. Good boy. Sit. Stay...

I thank Pam York for being in the right place at the right time to direct Miley away from potential euthanasia.
I thank Monica Blue for Cosette and for her part in the story of Miley. Without her I would not have had either,

and my life would have been so much the poorer for not knowing them. I also thank her for persistently trying to improve the health of this breed we love so much.

I thank Sally Gerlinger, who recognized my deep connection with Miley and understood that we were meant to be together. She kept Lucky/Jasmine/Miley safe for a week while Marty came to his senses. Without that Miles would have been lost to me forever.

I thank Caleb-whose-name-means-dog for loving Miley, and for telling me he missed her. He inspires me to write because I want him to understand things in life early on so his path will be joyous. I want him to know that the pain we suffer is tempered by the love we experience and the lessons we are shown. I pray he will always be tender and kind to all and remember that the least lovable is the one who needs love the most.

And I thank his parents, Benj and Molly, for trusting Miley with their precious son when she first came to me and was still somewhat mysterious. Miley would have laid her life down for him, as would the others. I thank them for their support of my writing efforts.

I thank all the wonderful veterinarians I've known in my adult life. Dr. Bob Brophy, who spoke wise words at the right moments.Dr. "Aunt Patti" Prato, who truly felt my connection with Cosette, and again with Miley, and who gifted Miles with freedom from her painful hip.Dr. Laurie Kelly, who sat and cried with me as I said goodbye to my beloved Pete and Macho horses. Because of her wisdom, I hope to always be the last image my dear pets see. Dr. Joe Melnarik, whose calm manner is a godsend in an emergency, and who showed me things are not always as bad as they seem. Dr. Linda Perry who helped me see more clearly who Miley really was.

I especially thank my friend, Dr. Hans Boer. For eleven years we have been partners in my dogs' health. He puts up with my odd requests, like headphones on Cosette so she could subconsciously hear my voice while being spayed. And what he teasingly calls my "voodoo" medicine, while acknowledging it is effective and complementary to his treatments, and occasionally recommending my treatment to others. He has generously given me advice, some of which I've actually followed, and explanations, and input when I need it. He has been there for the absolute lowest moments in my life, the losses of both Cosette and Miley, reassuring me that I was doing the right thing at the right time. We've also shared the joy of saving Sophie, and laughing about her post-Parvo, joy-of-life-ADHD. And Marty and my stay at the Boer B & B, where there is neither B nor B. I thank him for all his good work, and for recognizing my deep love of and devotion to my dogs.

I thank my friend Mary for honoring me by allowing me to share her loss of Cedar with her. I thank her for taking care of me and crying with me as we shared the loss of Miley. I thank her for her friendship in both good and bad times, and for courageously teaching "Canine Cuisine", and "Herbs and Homeopathy" with me. And for the wind chimes that brought noise back when it was so silent. I also thank her for patiently reading this book repeatedly and listening to me talk about it adnauseum until I thought I got it right. Her support was a gift to me. We may be "only children", but we are not alone.

I thank my sweet and generous niece Cheri Notti, an award-winning advanced English teacher, who painstakingly went through this book and made suggestions and corrections so I didn't look like a grammatical fool. I'm not sure how I've managed to get this age with no understanding of the functional use of a comma, but I'm grateful to know and love someone who does. I thank her for all her good words and encouragement. And for taking care of me and learning to make holistic dog food for my canine kids when I was "broken". I so appreciate her good Italian heart!

I thank my good friend Jean Atthowe, the 2002 winner of the Ken Shughart Humanitarian Award for starting the Montana Spay/Neuter Task Force. Jean expressed a desire to read my little manuscript and I sent it to her. Had I known her credentials as a retired Rutgers University English professor I would never have had the nerve to let her see it, but now I am so grateful I did! I thank her for proofing this book and for teaching me about dangling participles and split infinitives. And I praise her cause: www.mtspayneutertaskforce.org

I thank my talented photographer friend Debbie Hamilton for taking my very amateur photographs and turning them into works of art so that Miley's book would look as beautiful as she actually was.

I thank Joanne and Ralph Duncan for Sophie and Angus and for the wisdom they used in placing them with us. I am grateful for their hospitality in allowing us to stay with them while we made sure we chose the puppy who believed she could mend my broken heart. Sophie's work continues. She is my best friend, my business partner, my soul sister. We are as one spirit in two bodies.

I thank my friends Chris Whitehair, Debbie Hamilton, and Darlene Jevning who thought of my dogs when it came time to clean out their freezers or share their abundance. They provided me with beautiful meats to make holistic dog foods out of while saving us a lot of money. Their generosity has helped to keep my dog-kids healthy and happy.

I thank JoAnn and Trista for wanting to be our daughters, and for loving and babysitting for our beloved dogs when we needed them. These young women experienced unconditional love from us and from our dogs and are making us proud with their good characters.

I thank all my friends who understand my love for animals and share it. We have felt each other's joys and sorrows, sending prayers, cards, and emails of support back and forth. I thank Cindy Nicholls for crying with me and for sharing great food when I didn't want to eat. I thank my great hands-on therapeutic friends, Vicki Allsop and Betty Chisholm, who have worked hard to put my Humpty Dumpty heartbroken self back together again after this devastating loss. I thank the women at Animals Apawthecary for their sympathy and their herbal cancer formula to help me stage a battle to fight for Miley. .

And I also thank my friends who don't understand my love for animals but who saw my sorrow and tried to sympathize as best they could. Their efforts, no matter how awkward, did not go unnoticed or unappreciated. Be assured that all a person really has to do to comfort a friend is to care enough to be still and listen. That was an art Miley had perfected.

I thank Sophie (Voyager to My Heart), Angus (Voyager to My Soul), and the Empress Toots Anne Fullerton for generously sharing their home and their "parents" with a bedraggled little red waif that their mom fell in love with. I am grateful they were gentle and welcoming to Miley. They innately knew we were all a family. I'm so very proud of them.

And most importantly, I thank Miss Miley Anne Fullerton, PhD (Professional house Dog), for loving me with every fiber of her being. If I could have AKC registered her, the name I'd have chosen would have been 'Voyager to My Spirit'. She may have had a rough start, but she was loved by a kindly God who, I believe, providentially saw to it she came to me to be my teacher because I was open to giving my heart to the task of learning. I don't know what I ever did to deserve such a blessing, but I will be _forever grateful_.

References

For more information on homeopathy or to find a practitioner in your area you may contact:

www.NationalCenterForHomeopathy.org

Homeopathy has a long history of well-written books. There is a book out there for every level of learning, from the very basic to the professional. My two favorite beginner books are listed below. There are also very good schools such as the Homeopathy School International for the more seriously interested in homeopathic healing.

Everybody's Guide to Homeopathic Medicines
by Dana Ullman

The Complete Guide to Homeopathy
by Dr. Andrew Lockie

For more information on herbs refer to:
Everything You Ever Wanted to Know about Herbs For Pets by Mary Wulff and Greg Tilford

For herbal animal formulas go to:
www.animalsapawthecary.com

If you are interested in contacting me personally for more information on the art and science of homeopathy or for a phone consultation for yourself or your animals, you may write to me at:

21st Century Homeopathy

Jeanie E.A. Notti-Fullerton, cHom

1025 Cherry Orchard Loop

Hamilton, MT 59840

Or email me at:

cosettesmom@msn.com   putting in the subject line "Interest in Homeopathy" or "About Miley"

The Providential Doberman

Copyright 2012 by
Jeanie E. A. Notti-Fullerton

Made in the USA
Lexington, KY
27 February 2013